THE
FLOWER GARDEN

THE
FLOWER GARDEN

RICHARD BISGROVE

Photographs by Marijke Heuff

WINDWARD · FRANCES LINCOLN

A FRANCES LINCOLN BOOK

The Flower Garden
© Frances Lincoln Limited 1989
Text © Richard Bisgrove 1989
Photographs © Marijke Heuff 1989

The Flower Garden was conceived, edited and designed by
Frances Lincoln Limited, Apollo Works, 5 Charlton Kings Road, London NW5 2SB

WINDWARD
an imprint owned by W H Smith and Son Limited
Registered No. 237811, England
Trading as WHS Distributors
St. John's House, East Street, Leicester LE1 6NE

1 3 5 7 9 8 6 4 2

ISBN 0-7112-0522-1

Printed and bound in Italy by Lito Terrazzi

CONTENTS

INTRODUCTION

'Those who do not know are apt to think that flower gardening of the best kind is easy. It is not easy at all. It has taken me half a lifetime merely to find out what is best worth doing, and a good slice of another half to puzzle out the ways of doing it.'

When Gertrude Jekyll, the greatest artist-gardener of this century, wrote these words eighty years ago she was not trying to discourage amateurs. She was remonstrating against casual visitors to her garden who assumed that the effects they saw were due merely to luck and good soil. Most true gardeners are likely to fall into the opposite trap, of thinking that gardening, especially flower gardening 'of the best kind' is so difficult to achieve that they had better stick to tried and tested routines. This is sad, because so many opportunities are lost. Flower gardening is only difficult if one is determined to be right the first time, to gain experience without making mistakes, an impossible task in any endeavour.

To the beginner, mustering the necessary know-ledge, skills and co-ordination even to begin creating a flower garden can seem an impossible task; but with a few simple ground rules one makes a shaky start, and within a surprisingly short time the basics are mastered. Some people are then content to remain at a level of basic competence for ever, but the more adventurous set themselves higher and higher goals. Miss Jekyll was a gardener of this kind. She spent much of her life striving to perfect her techniques, and that is why she became so rightfully indignant when her hard-won results were attributed to good fortune.

This book is written for adventurous – but not necessarily knowledgeable – gardeners, those who are keen to have a beautiful flower garden, willing to devote a modicum of effort (physical and mental) to achieving their aims, and philosophical enough to view the occasional failure as a step towards the next success. No amount of reading can substitute for practical experience, but, as Miss Jekyll pointed out, it took her half a lifetime to find out what was best worth doing before she was able to tackle the problem of how to do it: phrasing the question was more difficult than providing the answer.

One aim of *The Flower Garden* is to short-circuit the learning process, to show what is possible and what might be desirable in varied circumstances. Because the scope for grouping flowers into beautiful gardens is limitless, I have included a few plans of successful gardens that I have designed, in order to illustrate how general principles can be translated into practice. It is not intended that the descriptions be regarded as a recipe book. Rather, I hope to show how particular flower gardens have arisen in response to particular circumstances so that the idea can be interpreted to suit your own circumstances – the situation of your garden, the climatic conditions, soil and so on.

In a hectic world, a garden offers a private refuge, with opportunities for relaxed outdoor living, for refreshment and an enforced change of pace from everyday life (a garden cannot be hurried), and for the expression of creativity. Each of us can decide what sort of garden best suits our personality, our budget and our surroundings, and set out to achieve such a garden. We can toy with the fascinating patterns of formal knots, revel in the glow of brilliant and inventive bedding schemes, explore the charms of diaphanous annuals, indulge in flower arranging, experiment with gardening as a fine art, or laze in the paradise of a *relatively* labour-saving garden. It is up to the individual to decide what sort of garden he or she wants. Every garden is, or should be, unique.

The successful flower garden depends on simplicity, harmony and breadth of effect. On the terraces at Hester-combe, the Jekyll garden in Somerset, stately spires of delphiniums in the fore-ground and background are carefully grouped into masses that echo the vertical lines of the balustrade. The soft grey foliage and crystalline white flowers of *Cerastium tomentosum* drape over the wall, softening but not obscuring the architecture and blending into the softer blues of the delphiniums. A solitary *Cistus × cyprius* below the balustrade repeats the white of the cerastium, to complete the unity of the picture.

A SETTING FOR FLOWERS

A fundamental principle behind creating a flower garden can be summarized in the all-embracing advice of eighteenth-century writers to 'consult the genius of the place in all': use the idiosyncrasies of the site to create a unique garden; choose plants appropriate to the particular soil and situation of the garden rather than struggling to grow hybrid tea roses on thin gravel or rhododendrons on chalk or limestone.

The tradition of gardening is based on growing plants that do well in open, sunny situations and in fertile, deeply cultivated soil. Most modern gardening books perpetuate this approach, but there are flowering plants suitable for almost any soil and situation so it is wiser to think first how people might like to use the garden before deciding what to plant and where.

Recognizing the genius of the place will help to suggest where one might like to sit in the garden, which parts of the garden will be seen every day and which hardly at all, where views might be captured or should be lost – and hence what sort of enclosure is desirable. The aspect of the garden will have a major influence on how it is used.

SUN, SOIL AND ASPECT

Most gardens, especially small ones, are places of extremes. The soil may be heavy clay over most of the garden with a dry strip adjacent to the house. In other districts the soil may be sandy and dry except for patches where water running off driveways increases the local 'rainfall' to three or four times the normal. Part of the garden will be in heavy shade from the house and possibly from fences and trees, while on the other side of the house the soil may be baked by the sun. Of course improvements can be made to the soil by using manure, peat or other bulky organic materials to assist in plant establishment, but to go to great lengths to eliminate all the variations in the garden in order to grow the same demanding plants everywhere is clearly an expensive folly. It makes much more sense to capitalize on the diversity of both soil and aspect, growing sun- and shade-tolerant plants in opposite corners of the garden, for example, and thus to create a garden which truly 'consults the genius of the place in all.'

Take time to consider the aspect and how this will relate to the use you make of your garden. For instance, when the main garden-front of the house receives the midday or afternoon sun there will be a sheltered and usually rather dry area against the house where many interesting and aromatic plants could be grown. This warm spot is also an obvious place for a paved garden, a terrace or patio, where one might sit in comfort even in mild midwinter spells. Plants arching over the windows of the house to furnish the paved garden and soften its link with the house will also shield rooms from the midday sun in summer, whereas low winter light will spill unimpeded into the house.

In contrast, the end of the garden – the main view from the house – will be largely in shade, not the ideal aspect for flowering plants, but a careful choice of flowers (especially white flowers) and good foliage will hide the true limits of the garden in the

When creating a flower garden it is important to consider the surroundings – where views should be captured or lost – and where it might be pleasant to sit. In this leafy setting, the greenish-white flowers of *Aruncus sylvester*, white shrub roses and floribundas and the spires of white foxgloves around an open lawn combine to create a cool summer retreat. The variegated leaves of hostas and grasses echo the dappled sunlight filtering through the trees.

mysterious depths of the border's shadows. If the leafy end of the garden includes plants with good autumn foliage, the sun shining through the leaves into the garden will display the translucent beauty of autumn tints to the full.

A shaded aspect to the garden-front of the house might appear less favourable at first glance, but it does mean that the end of the garden, the main view from the house, will be bright and sunny and that the surprising number of flowers which turn towards the sun will be shown to best advantage in that view. In cool climates the warmest corner of the garden, well away from the house, provides a logical place for a paved garden with seats and perhaps a table, an attractive focal point when seen from the house and an invitation to use the garden. The patio itself could be introspective in character, immersed in the surrounding planting, or could look back to the house framed in greenery. By using the shaded ground near

In this shady clearing, a simple planting of pale azaleas, bluebells and cow parsley emphasizes the woodland character. Spotted-leaved pulmonarias and the glossy fountains of colchicum foliage promise flowers at other seasons, and combine with pale ferns to enhance the natural breadth of the scene. One small red azalea by the path picks up the warmer colouring of the tall rhododendrons that merge into the dark of trees.

the house for ferns, hostas, foxgloves, trilliums and other woodlanders, the shade border will provide an effective foreground to the sunny garden beyond and, of course, a delightful feature in itself. Many shrubs and climbers are also suitable for a shady wall. Our kitchen window, which only receives the morning sun, is surrounded by *Azara dentata,* covered in late spring with powder puff yellow flowers: the bright evergreen leaves of the azara catch the sun's rays and reflect them into the kitchen long after the direct sunlight has ceased to play on the window.

A SHADE BORDER

Much interest can be created with foliage alone in a shaded border but, in the narrow bed under an old apple tree opposite our kitchen window we wanted some flowers at least in the early part of the year. In summer, when the courtyard as a whole is sunnier, plants in pots provide most of the colour.

Foliage is important, of course, so the edge of the border is planted with irregular drifts of *Asarum europaeum, Cyclamen neapolitanum* and *Liriope muscari* with various epimediums behind and one or two good evergreen ferns. The epimediums, too, are effectively evergreen, retaining their old burnished leaves through the winter, but in this border most of the old leaves are cut off at ground level early in the new year.

The main flowering season starts with snowdrops and aconites among the fresh young leaves of *Arum italicum* var. *pictum* but scattered plants of Lent hellebores, chosen for their greenish white, pale pink and deep maroon colouring, soon add to the effect with their expanding flowers. The deeper colours associate with the deep red colour of the few remaining clumps of epimedium foliage. By early spring the epimediums themselves begin to flower, their graceful uncoiling stems bearing flowers of white, red and cream just ahead of the almost equally beautiful leaves. The baton passes, though, to two erythroniums, 'White Beauty' and *E. tuolumnense* 'Pagoda', surviving remarkably well and creating a wonderful effect of woodland charm among the fresh green foliage of aconites, arums and ferns, even though the woodland stretches only 5 × 1m/16 × 3ft or so.

By late spring the bulb foliage is dying away and the erythroniums disappear with amazing rapidity, but the remains are covered by expanding carpets of epimediums and the quite aggressive domes of handsome hellebore leaves. In spring a single plant of *Paeonia mlokosewitschii,* so frail in appearance but so tough in constitution, steals the limelight and the season continues into midsummer with the pale yellow *Digitalis ambigua* and a solitary white *Lilium martagon,* refusing to increase beyond the one bulb originally bought but thankfully also refusing to die.

Even in early summer the border is beginning to look jaded as the apple tree takes most of the water from the already dry soil, so we are pleased to distract attention with pots of summer annuals. It always comes as a pleasant surprise when, in early autumn, the first flowers of the cyclamen appear, followed by the dull purple spikes of liriope and the cyclamen's own lovely foliage, warning that the first snowdrops are not far off.

In a larger shade border there would be scope for many more plants, more hellebores, interesting ivies and euphorbias, Solomon's seal, geraniums, pulmonarias and perhaps the thuggish symphytums. Even in this small border it would be possible to squeeze in some variegated honesty, some white lamium in the foreground and the lovely snake's head fritillaries, which survive, even if they do not spread very rapidly, only a short distance away in the garden. However, the white variegations would be too bright for our woodland effect and too many different plants would spoil the sense of breadth of this tiny area.

1 *Garrya elliptica*
2 *Helleborus orientalis*
3 Apple tree
4 Fern
5 Arums with snowdrops and aconites
6 *Asarum europaeum*
7 *Epimedium × rubrum*
8 *Digitalis ambigua*
9 *Cyclamen neapolitum*
10 *Lilium martagon* 'Album'
11 *Erythronium* 'White Beauty' and *E. tuolumnense* 'Pagoda'
12 *Liriope muscari*
13 *Epimedium × warleyense*
14 *Paeonia mlokosewitschii*
15 *Epimedium × versicolor* 'Sulphureum'

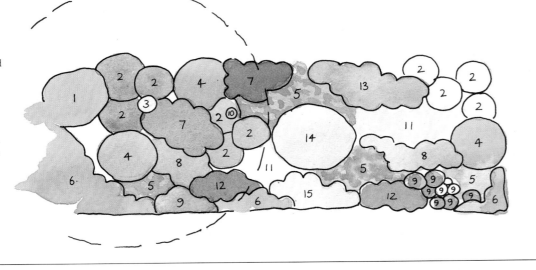

GARDEN CHARACTER

Gardens can be geometrical, with symmetrical patterns of straight lines, circles and spirals filled with uniform masses of bedding plants. They may be regular, perhaps with rectangular lawns, straight paths and box-hedged beds and borders, accentuated with topiary, seats and other architectural features, but with the planting as a whole softly informal.

More commonly, the garden may be arranged but informal. There is a clear distinction between lawns, paving and borders but their shapes are irregularly serpentine, inspired by the eighteenth-century landscape garden. On a large scale, sweeping curves may carry the eye out to unite the garden with distant hills or rounded groups of trees, but too often the desire to create a 'natural' garden within a small rectangular plot has unnatural results, as the cramped twistings and turnings are for ever colliding with the garden boundary.

Sometimes the shapes within the garden, whether regular or meandering, will be dissolved one into another by blurring the edges. Borders spill out over paths, with outlying tufts of plants growing in the path itself; the path merges into the lawn by virtue of its irregular edge, perhaps with paving stones extending into the lawn, and the hard junction between horizontal surfaces and vertical walls is softened by climbers on the walls and by bold planting at their base. Scandinavian garden designers in particular

LEFT Hedges, clipped greens and a large flower pot gently underline the formal character of this garden, but plants are arranged informally within the rectangular borders. In one border yellow and white flowers pick up the pale colours of background foliage; soft pinks, mauves and greys are grouped in the other. The result is greater variety of effect than would be achieved by mixing the colours indiscriminately.

RIGHT Charming annual flowers hide garden paths and boundaries in an informal sea of planting, with sweet peas climbing into the shrubby surroundings to complete the effect. Among the indistinct forms of the annuals, patches of scarlet zinnias and orange marigolds, with spikes of antirrhinums, accentuate the otherwise pastel scheme.

Skilful changes in level and the partial enclosure of a handsome pergola shape this garden into a sheltered bowl. Formal panels of grass, carefully detailed stone edges and large beds filled to overflowing with bold groups of peonies, delphiniums and lilies are beautifully woven together. Roses, iris, catmint and clematis on the higher levels echo the soft colouring of the central sunken garden. The planting scheme, designed by Gertrude Jekyll, is at its most colourful for midsummer but the edging of bergenias, clumps of grasses and the brilliant geometry of Edwin Lutyens' architecture ensure that the garden never lacks interest.

HISTORICAL INSPIRATION

This small garden set on one level and separated from the village street by a high stone wall provides the setting for a charming nineteenth-century gothic style house. Its owners recognized that their own first love, the informal cottage garden, might literally swamp the architectural quality of the house and sought a treatment that would reflect its character. Realizing that the house itself borrowed from history by looking back to medieval building styles, they have used the trefoil shape of the windows as the basis of a simple geometrical pattern and created a garden that is part medieval knot, part formal bedding, but with a softness to the mass planting more suited to their own leanings.

Within low box hedges, the four main quarters of the bed are planted with 'Little White Pet', a dwarf, fragrant and perpetual flowering rose dating back to 1879, with *Viola cornuta* to fill the interstices. The four small triangles are planted with *Artemisia splendens,* a froth of grey, wiry leaves in summer but with a poor winter appearance. In late autumn, therefore, the artemisia is cut to the ground, allowing white crocus to appear in spring. In summer, the dainty white *Fuchsia* 'Ting-a-Ling' is planted into each of the triangles to hover over the rejuvenated silvery foliage.

With interest created in the knot for most of the summer, the two narrow borders beneath the house and the outer wall are used for winter, late spring and autumn flowers. Against the house, the shadier of the two borders houses *Sarcococca hookeriana digyna, Daphne odora* 'Aureo-marginata' and a few good clumps of purple *Helleborus orientalis.* All of these pick up the warm pink-grey tints in the stone while adding solemnity and weight with their dark foliage. Irregular groups of these few plants along the whole of the border create a feeling of unity and variety, but the effect is prevented from becoming too sombre by interspersing drifts of snowdrops and spotted-leaved pulmonarias. In the sunnier border beneath the outer wall, seen from one of the most important windows in the house, the grey stone is used as a backdrop for soft grey-green foliage and purple-pink flowers: *Daphne × burkwoodii, Syringa meyeri* 'Palibin' and, on the wall, *Clematis macropetala* for spring; *Fuchsia magellanica* 'Versicolor', *Caryopteris × clandonensis* and *Clematis viticella* in autumn with a ground cover of *Bergenia purpurascens, Berberis thunbergii* 'Atropurpurea Nana' and narrow-leaved, plum-scented *Iris graminea* to anchor the otherwise overdelicate scheme. A single plant of *Paeonia mlokosewitschii* adds its exquisitely beautiful single flowers of pale yellow to complement the spring plants for the week or so that the peony lasts – a fleeting but memorable detail.

This simple pattern could have been planted with perennial plants only, forgetting the nicety of tender fuchsias and risky artemisias. It could have been bedded more solidly, with purple petunias or deep purple heliotrope and fountains of silvery *Senecio bicolor cineraria,* or with pale yellow petunias within a lavender hedge (given the subtle colouring of the wall), and violas and pale tulips or soft yellow wallflowers in spring, but the balance of solidity and change, the softness of the many-petalled roses and freedom of violas trailing across the firm shapes of the box suited the owners best.

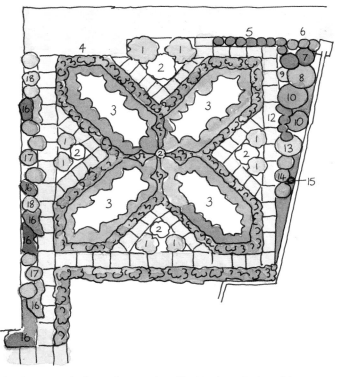

1 *Artemisia splendens* and crocus (white)
2 *Fuchsia* 'Ting-a-Ling'
3 *Rosa* 'Little White Pet' edged with *Viola cornuta*
4 Box hedges
5 *Liriope muscari*
6 *Bergenia purpurascens*
7 *Berberis thunbergii* 'Atropurpurea Nana'
8 *Fuchsia magellanica* 'Versicolor'
9 *Paeonia mlokosewitschii*
10 *Daphne × burkwoodii*
11 *Clematis macropetala*
12 *Iris graminea*
13 *Syringa meyeri* 'Palibin'
14 *Caryopteris × clandonensis*
15 *Clematis viticella*
16 *Helleborus orientalis, Pulmonaria saccharata* and snowdrops
17 *Sarcococca hookeriana digyna*
18 *Daphne odora* 'Aureo-marginata'

seem to have mastered the art of clothing paved surfaces with naturalistic plant associations without obscuring the design.

At the extreme, shapes may disappear altogether from the ground pattern as the garden takes on a jungle-like profusion, with open spaces irregularly distributed through the plant mass and plants intruding into every open space, whether in a tiny, luxuriantly planted courtyard garden or in a large woodland garden where paths meander seemingly at random through the undergrowth.

Within this range of garden character from regimented to rugged, the nature of the planting can also vary, from bold forms, colours and textures to delicate; using one colour or having separate colour schemes in different parts of the garden, or having a complete mixture or gradation of colour, or perhaps ringing the changes from season to season.

More than anything else, it is the relationship between open space and solid planting that determines the character of the garden. Although the treatment of boundaries between them is infinitely variable, the extremes of uncluttered open space and dense planting should always be evident in the garden. Rather than looking for an empty space in which to show off each new plant in splendid

LEFT In a small, rectangular garden it makes sense to accept rather than fight against the boundaries. In this garden, informal drifts of flowers soften the geometry and partially obscure the attractive silver-grey fence. Strong forms of iris and grasses in the narrow border on the left balance the larger masses of the main flower border. The fence wraps round to conceal the furthest extent of the garden and a cascade of white roses accentuates the mysterious blackness against which the focal point is displayed.

RIGHT The shade beneath the branches of arching shrubs can be used as a background for brightly illuminated flowers. Here, white spires of lupins and delphiniums, flat plates of yellow achilleas, and other pale flowers, are accentuated by background shadows.

isolation, it is preferable to look for suitable neighbours to associate with the newcomer. Flowers are more telling when concentrated into groups: individual flowers will then enhance each other, providing harmonies and contrasts of colour and form, and the group of flowers will form a focal point against what then becomes a substantial green background.

CREATING A BACKGROUND

If there is a general rule for creating a flower garden it should be to leave the centre of the garden open and to plant around the edges of the open space. Pushing flowers to the edges of the garden usually means that various borders have different aspects, offering scope for the cultivation of a wide range of plants. This variation, not only of the plants but also of the way they are illuminated by the sun, creates a garden of more interest and real variety and greatly simplifies maintenance.

Light has an important effect on the way that colours are seen. In cold climates the hazy atmosphere and often grey skies dazzle the eye, in effect 'overexposing' the garden picture and bleaching colours. Flowers are infinitely more effective when seen against a background than when silhouetted against the sky. In the clearer light of warmer regions, flower colours show up brilliantly against reliably blue skies, but the intense heat of summer is such that the garden spectator can best appreciate the brilliance from the shady retreat provided by background planting.

Slender trails of clematis enhance rather than conceal the massive buttresses of a retaining wall. Alstroemerias revel in the sheltered border at the base of the wall, reaching up and mingling with the clematis, and forming dense, spreading colonies increasing in beauty year by year.

Flowering climbers and wall plants

Sometimes walls and fences create sufficient enclosure for the flower garden but they require softening with climbing plants and wall-shrubs. For this purpose, evergreen or the more substantial deciduous plants are better than slender climbers that leave a tangled mass of thin stems in the winter.

On a sheltered sunny wall the opportunities are endless. *Clematis cirrhosa balearica* has glossy evergreen foliage, elegantly cut and bronzing attractively in the winter to set off its charming white flowers to perfection. *Wisteria sinensis* is an obvious choice for early summer, deciduous but attractive in the pale grey of its picturesque branching habit in winter, and often carrying a smaller second crop of flowers in late summer. The climbing solanums, *S. crispum* and *S. jasminoides* 'Album', flower for several months in late summer and, in a sheltered position, keep much of their dark, glossy foliage during the winter. *Jasminum officinale,* too, is semi-evergreen and, left unpruned, soon develops into large swags, laden with heavily scented white flowers in the summer. Honeysuckle flourishes in full sunlight but does not demand such luxury, and its peeling brown leafless stems in winter are attractive, if rather untidy.

For shady walls the choice is more limited but no less beautiful. *Clematis montana* grows rapidly, flowers with immense freedom and soon produces a mass of interwoven twigs to mask walls and provide a haven for small birds. The pink forms such as *C.m.* 'Rosea' and the deeper 'Tetrarose' are most commonly seen, but the ordinary species, which has white flowers and a delightful vanilla scent, is more versatile and shows up especially well in dark corners. *Hydrangea petiolaris* is invaluable in shade, climbing infuriatingly slowly at first, but producing white lace-cap flowers with great freedom on handsomely branching plants in early summer. The leaves colour well in autumn and fall to reveal stems covered in peeling, orange-brown bark. *Pileostegia viburnoides* is quite rare, not because it is difficult but because it belongs to the more leisurely past when people were prepared to wait for their gardens to develop. Its long, glossy green leaves on self-clinging stems eventually make a handsome and trouble-free plant covered in late summer and autumn with creamy white flowers.

With both the hydrangea and pileostegia it is wise to combine them with faster-growing climbers such as clematis and honeysuckle for the first few years, taking care that the more permanent plants are given room to develop.

No companion climbers are needed with winter jasmine, *Jasminum nudiflorum,* as it grows so quickly, its arching green stems decked in bright yellow flowers in early and midwinter. It rapidly develops into an untidy heap unless the stems that have flowered are removed, leaving young new shoots in their place. It is a long, thin shrub rather than a true climber and needs to be tied in to wires or trained to grow on a trellis.

Winter jasmine introduces a whole range of 'wall-shrubs', a loose term which embraces plants that are too lax to support themselves, those that need the shelter provided by a wall, and also plants that are often grown up against a wall even though they would grow well as free-standing shrubs.

Viburnum × *bodnantense* and *Chimonanthus praecox* are two such shrubs. Both flower in winter, the viburnum from the beginning of winter and chimonanthus at the end. The flowers benefit from the protection afforded by a sunny wall and the scent will be more noticeable in a sheltered spot. The chimonanthus also produces its flower buds more freely in such a situation. Quince (*Chaenomeles* × *superba*) is another plant that grows well in the open, making a wide spreading shrub 1m/3ft or so tall, but trained on a wall it flowers earlier and more freely and reaches a height of 2-3m/7-10ft or more if desired. Its brilliant orange, crimson, pink or white flowers are produced on leafless branches so a careful match of each variety to its background is essential. Ceanothus, especially the beautiful *C. impressus,* the silky-leaved *Cytisus battandieri,* with its pineapple scented yellow flowers, *Fremontodendron californicum,* rushing up stiffly to 3-4m/10-14ft before dying in a harder than average

perhaps centuries, eventually reaching the eaves of three-storey buildings.

All these plants are intended to clothe walls and fences and to some extent to soften outlines by growing over the top. Many more plants will flourish in the sheltered conditions at the base of a wall to soften the angularity of its junction with the ground. Fuchsias, hebes, the beautiful tender buddlejas, *Coronilla glauca* with its pleasant habit of flowering in autumn as well as spring, daphnes and many others may be used. Against shady walls, *Skimmia japonica*, *Sarcococca ruscifolia* and *S. hookeriana digyna*, the very early flowering *Daphne pontica* and *D. laureola*, mahonias and *Ribes laurifolium*, an elegant currant producing racemes of greenish white flowers among evergreen foliage in midwinter, are excellent plants and most of them produce their sweetly scented flowers in winter and early spring.

For summer, the range of 'anchoring' plants is wider still. Alstroemeria never look better than when bursting from the base of a wall. The romneyas, tree peonies, *Phygelius aequalis* and *P. capensis* also look splendid in such a location, although the last-named can be rather invasive. Valerian *(Centranthus ruber)*, in its white, pink and deep red forms, looks especially attractive and, if allowed to spread, the small seedlings that spring from crevices in steps, paving and even the wall itself, help to unify the garden.

Where the enclosure is not adequate, it can be reinforced by trellis and pillars with lighter plants such as clematis of all kinds, including the slender viticellas and large-flowered hybrids, and roses with their long season of often fragrant flowers. Wisteria is particularly lovely when its pendant racemes can swing freely from a pergola or similar open structure while honeysuckle and summer jasmine are amenable to letting go or cutting hard back to create just the degree of enclosure required.

Where decoration and flowers are more important than structure, annual or nearly annual climbers also have much to offer, especially when some effect is needed in a hurry. *Eccremocarpus scaber* survives mild winters to grow like a more or less herbaceous

winter and covered in clear yellow flowers for the whole summer, all benefit from the protection of a wall in full sunlight but will amply repay their rent with handsome evergreen foliage as well as flowers freely produced. Given space, *Magnolia grandiflora* is an even more handsome shrub, taking its time to flower even if one chooses one of the selected clones such as 'Goliath' or 'Exmouth', but unlike the quick-growing, quick-dying ceanothus, cytisus and fremontodendron, it will survive for decades,

RIGHT Where enclosure is
lacking in the garden it is easily
achieved by growing
flowering climbers up light
supports. Wisteria, with its
beautiful, fragrant flowers, is
ideal. Its grey-green leaves
create attractive patterns
against the sky and the
tortuous, silver-grey stems are
seen to better effect winding
round a post than when trained
flat against a wall.

LEFT Where decoration is more
important than density, annual
climbers provide a charming
and speedy solution. Slender
trails of canary creeper, with
elegant foliage and prettily
fringed flowers, emphasize the
rigid geometry of their metal
support by their own free
growth and add to the screen
without being oppressive.
Sweet peas are coarser in leaf,
but have the advantage of a
wide colour range and delicate
perfume.

perennial but is safer treated as a half-hardy annual. The bright orange-scarlet tubular flowers are particularly effective against red-brick walls; the paler yellow and red forms look good against stone, wood and many painted surfaces. The runner bean, so invaluable as a vegetable, was first introduced into Europe as a flowering plant and, in its scarlet, pink and white flowered forms, could still be much more widely used as an ornamental plant. Climbing nasturtiums and the more refined canary creeper *(Tropaeolum peregrinum)* are also excellent for quick effect. Both are susceptible to black-fly and caterpillar damage so a careful watch needs to be kept for these pests as plants stunted by severe attacks will take a long time to recover. The lovely morning glory and intriguing *Rhodochiton volubile*, with its purple-crimson calyx and almost black-crimson tubular flowers, need warm conditions and in cool climates

are best grown in pots or planted out from pots.

Beautiful as they are individually, many of the climbers look even better with suitable partners. Deep red roses such as 'Compassion', 'Climbing Etoile de Hollande' and the single flowered 'Altissimo' provide excellent support, both physically and visually, for *Clematis viticella* and its hybrids and for purple or lavender large-flowered clematis such as 'Lasurstern' (early flowering), 'Ascotiensis' or 'Perle d'Azur', or the very long-flowering, deep purple 'The President'. Yellow and copper roses also look wonderful with such companions. White clematis growing up through the larger grey-leaved shrubs such as *Cytisus battandieri* and *Abutilon vitifolium* have an ethereal quality which is not achieved by seeing the flowers among their own green foliage, while purple-leaved grape and the velvety-leaved *Parthenocissus henryana* add a sumptuous richness to the

LEFT Clematis and other slender climbers can be allowed to scramble over shrubs to create harmonious colour combinations. Pale clematis and grey-leaved lavender make delightful partners, especially where the lavender is planted near steps down which the clematis can tumble.

RIGHT Weaving two or three climbers over a pillar or other support extends the tapestry effect of a flower garden into the third dimension. Here, delicate sprays of creamy white *Clematis recta* and pale pink *Rosa* 'New Dawn' intermingle in a fine-textured blend of soft colours.

Hydrangea petiolaris is one of the best climbers for a shaded situation, and is self-clinging on rough brickwork. Its white lace-cap flowers bring light into dark corners and the wide-branching habit creates a mosaic of light green foliage and deep shadows, further alleviating the gloom. Spent flower heads fade to a warm brown, remaining on the plant throughout the winter to echo the colour of its shaggy-barked stems. Against a background of brick and faded timber the effect is particularly rugged and handsome.

flowers of *Clematis viticella,* its deep red hybrid *C.* 'Kermesina', and the common but no less valuable 'Jackmanii Superba'. One of the most beautiful, subtle and delicate combinations I have ever seen was the large, single rose 'Meg' with the tiny high-pointed buds of 'Bloomfield Abundance' interlaced with *Clematis* 'Nelly Moser'. The pink bars on the petals of 'Nelly Moser', fading as the flowers aged, matched the slightly different pinks of the two roses as they, too, changed and the sudden discovery of the charming, miniature buds of 'Bloomfield Abundance' among the much larger flowers of its two partners provided constant delight.

Self-clinging climbers such as ivy, pileostegia and the various *Parthenocissus* species also provide useful support for scrambling plants. Tall nasturtiums climbing up through dark-leaved ivy have an added brilliance because of their background and we have grown *Eccremocarpus scaber* through the self-supporting *Myrtus communis* with similar effect.

Climbers and wall plants may be grown together to supplement the flowering season rather than to complement their flower colours. In one sheltered corner of our garden we grow *Buddleja auriculata* which produces small but very sweetly scented buff flowers throughout the winter on a vigorous shrub that has to be severely pruned and tied back to the wall to avoid blocking the doorway. The wires to which it is tied also support *Clematis macropetala,* with pale lavender flowers produced in great abundance in early summer (followed by silky seed heads which are still delightful in the autumn) and a superior form of *Lonicera sempervirens* which produces scarlet trumpet flowers for most of the summer. We are planning to add *Campsis radicans* which has much larger flowers of a similar colouring in late summer and autumn so that there will be something in flower all year round.

Care is needed in choosing partners that do not cause maintenance problems. Grapes and late clematis are easy because the grape is hard-pruned in late winter, at which time the clematis can be cut almost to ground level and the tops easily disentangled from the remaining rods of the vine. Roses, too, are hard-pruned in autumn and/or spring and their stiff remaining branches are easily strong enough to stand the tugging that is necessary to disentangle the surplus top-growth of the clematis. *Clematis montana* and honeysuckle can be pruned after flowering and disentangled as necessary, soon covering themselves with fresh growth to flower the following year.

Climbers and wall plants chosen for enclosure should also be chosen to suit the overall character of the garden and to accord with their neighbours. *Clematis macropetala* with its grey-green leaves and powder-blue flowers emerging from a sturdy mound of soft pink *Daphne × burkwoodii,* buff-cream honeysuckle sharing wall space with multicoloured alstroemerias below, or *Clematis viticella* trailing its purple flowers down to mingle with the red and purple globes of hardy fuchsias are far more effective than any of these plants seen in isolation.

Evergreens

In addition to the plants that enclose the flower garden, points of emphasis will be needed at strategic points, perhaps to frame a vista or reinforce the front edge of a border. Plants to create this backbone of the garden can be chosen entirely for their permanence – clipped box, yew or other evergreens strategically disposed. Also, there are plants that provide both structure and seasonal interest.

Evergreen shrubs for backbone planting need not be restricted to spotted aucubas and dark laurels, useful though these may be in many situations. The choice of good flowering evergreens ranges from aristrocratic eucryphias and tall rhododendrons on suitably acid soil to pyracanthas, *Arbutus unedo* and the handsome privet, *Ligustrum lucidum* on chalk. *Berberis × stenophylla* is so vigorous that it could get out of hand, and like all the berberis is painfully difficult to prune, but the warm orange of the species and the paler colours of its recently produced varieties, adored by bees in the spring, make them useful for large-scale planting. In more sheltered positions, *Garrya elliptica,* the papery-petalled *Cistus × cyprius,* and the two hardier azaras might be tried.

Azara microphylla has very small, dark green leaves and almost invisible flowers but with a powerful vanilla fragrance in late winter; *A. serrata* is larger, looser, pale green and flowers profusely in midsummer with powder puffs of bright yellow.

Evergreen interest may also be provided at a lower level. *Viburnum davidii,* the taller and much less common *V. cinnamomifolium* and *Skimmia japonica* are outstanding with their large, dark leaves and perfect, low-domed profile, so much so that one tends to forget that they are attractive flowering and fruiting shrubs too. Where polished perfection is not the aim, *Berberis candidula* and *Escallonia* 'Apple Blossom' may fit the bill. Both are much finer textured in leaf, much prettier in flower (orange in the case of the berberis, pale pink as the 'Apple Blossom' suggests) and have a slightly looser habit of growth.

The shrubby herbs, such as green, purple or yellow-variegated sage, cotton lavender (*Santolina*

Bergenias are invaluable for the backbone they provide among finer-textured foliage and flowers. In this scheme, the bold, polished leaves serve as a foil to the dusky-coloured flowers of sedums, betonica, dicentras, pinks and alliums.

chamaecyparissus), lavender and rosemary are also extremely useful, both in leaf and flower.

Perhaps the most varied small evergreens are the hebes. *Hebe anomala,* the hardiest, has small, dark green leaves and small white spikes of flower on a dome which can reach 2m/7ft high. *H. rakaiensis,* a refreshing bright, pale green, especially cheerful in the middle of winter, is also white flowered but less than 1m/3ft tall. *H. albicans* is lower still with waxy grey leaves that make it ideal for use in the grey garden, in contrast to the usually feathery growth of other grey-leaved plants, while *H. ochracea* looks more like a juniper than a hebe with its golden scale-like leaves on arching branches, and the flowers are borne in the leaf axils like a frosting over the plant. *H.* 'Amy', 'Autumn Glory', and the smaller leaved, smaller flowered 'Mrs Winder' and 'Bowles' Hybrid' are purple-leaved hebes with purple flowers.

At the lowest level, bergenias, with their huge, leathery, evergreen leaves, make excellent low accent points. They also flower early in the growing season when there is little else in flower. *Bergenia cordifolia,* whose leaves turn rich purple in the winter, has dumpy flower spikes of a lurid magenta pink, but these can be made more acceptable by associating them with the darker purple forms of *Helleborus orientalis* and the upright wands of *Daphne mezereum.* Alternatively, there are now many other bergenias with better flowers, clearer pink and much earlier in the case of *B.* × *schmidtii* and 'Profusion', a livelier deep crimson in the smaller *B. purpurascens* and a much taller, more elegant spire of white flowers fading to apple-blossom pink in 'Silberlicht'. In these improved flowered forms, though, the leafage is less dense and less dramatic.

FOLIAGE COLOUR

In the flower garden, shrubs with variegated or coloured foliage are particularly useful as they supplement and harmonize with the colour schemes created by the flowers, reinforcing the colour effects over a very long season.

Bronze and purple foliage

One of the most useful foliage colours for contributing to successful plant association is that variously described as copper, bronze or purple, the depth of colouring ranging from slightly bronze-tinted green to dark crimson-purple.

The darkest of all in this group must be the almost black-leaved *Ophiopogon planiscapus nigrescens,* a low-growing and slow-growing grassy tuft bearing insignificant purple-green flowers. Unlike most purple-leaved plants it seems to grow best in a shady situation, where its dark colour does not show up well, but it will grow in sunnier locations and makes

a stunning edge to a border of dark leaves and crimson flowers.

Cotinus coggygria, the smoke bush, is widely grown for its purple leaves. The one most readily available, 'Royal Purple' or 'Notcutt's Variety', has leaves of a deep reddish purple but the old 'Foliis Purpureis' should not be overlooked for its less heavy colouring and the species itself, with the most delightful glaucous green leaves, completes an excellent trio for use in large borders where gradation of flower and foliage colouring from crimson to pink and white is desired. The species also has the most spectacular autumn foliage. Other dark-leaved plants extend from copper beech and 'Crimson King' maple, both large trees which may be coppiced as shrubs for the back of a large border, through cotinus, purple hazel and purple plum to *Weigela florida* 'Foliis Purpureis' (best when hard-pruned after flowering to maintain its colour). Among herbaceous plants, *Sedum telephium maximum* 'Atropurpureum' at 60cm/24in, *Viola labradorica purpurea* at 15cm/6in and the ground-hugging *Sedum spurium* 'Purple Carpet' offer foliage of a dark hue with dusky pink flowers in autumn on the sedums and pale lavender flowers set off by the viola leaves in spring.

Also among the dark purples are several tender plants, formerly associated with foliage and carpet bedding but equally at home in the more relaxed environs of the abundant flower garden. *Perilla nankinensis* is the darkest of all, its crinkled, nettle-like leaves accentuating the depth of colouring, but *Iresine herbstii* and the very low alternantheras can be similarly employed. Cannas were important in the 'subtropical' foliage borders of the nineteenth century but they were also much appreciated by Gertrude Jekyll for the flower border and are being increasingly appreciated today, varying in leaf colour from deep purple through mildly bronze and bright green to brilliantly yellow-veined. Largest of all are the leaves of *Ricinus communis* 'Gibsonii', the purple-leaved castor oil plant, which given a favourable summer and good soil will easily grow from its large seed to 2m/7ft or more.

These dark foliage plants create a sumptuous effect with flowers of deep crimson, purple or fiery scarlet. They also contrast beautifully with paler pink, cream or white flowers. *Achillea* 'Moonshine', for example, against purple-leaved cotinus forms a wonderful picture for the whole of the summer. Care should be taken, though, when placing grey-leaved pale flowers against dark purple leaves, as the contrast is so complete that it gives the planting a blotchy appearance. The solution is to use various depths of foliage colour in the composition of the border rather than aiming always for maximum contrast.

Somewhat lighter in colour are the purple-leaved berberis, of which there are an ever-increasing number. *Berberis* × *ottawensis* 'Superba' is a tall shrub, 2m/7ft or more; *B. thunbergii atropurpurea* is commonly half that size while *B.t.* 'Atropurpurea Nana' is a compact mound of bright reddish-purple, with its dark stems effective even in winter. It is an excellent foreground plant among fuchsias, scarlet or crimson tulips and flowers of similar colouring. Grown from seed, *B.t. atropurpurea* is as variable in depth of colouring as purple beech so it is possible to select individuals for a colour-graded scheme. A fourth useful berberis, 'Rose Glow', is purple in its first flush of foliage but then produces leaves splashed with bright pink so the whole effect of the plant is light and frothy, ideal for associating with grey foliage and flowers of soft colouring.

Where a bold accent is called for, the purple forms of *Phormium tenax* and *Rheum palmatum* could hardly be bettered. At a lesser scale, *Heuchera americana,* with its beautiful satin leaf, and the newer, bolder *H. micrantha* 'Palace Purple' are admirable plants for the front of the border, the latter being especially delightful in late summer and autumn when it produces its innumerable off-white spikes of flowers. Even later in the year the charming white butterfly-like flowers of *Saxifraga fortunei* 'Wada's Form' appear, hovering over glossy purple-backed leaves and showing to best advantage in the cool, shaded position it requires.

Paler still are the bronze-tinted leaves of *Plantago major rubrifolia, Crocosmia* 'Solfatare', crimson sweet William and several of the dark-flowered polyanthus and primroses (Crimson Beauty, Ruby Port, Garryarde Guinevere). Finally, such plants as purple sage, *Rosa glauca* (better known as *R. rubrifolia)* and the graceful *Clematis recta* 'Purpurea' have purple-stained foliage with so much glaucous sheen that it is hard to decide whether the foliage is purple or grey. The distinction is not important, however, as a harmonious grouping of foliage varying from deepest purple to glaucous grey and silver forms a perfect setting and complements flowers of any colour.

RIGHT Bronze foliage adds richness to a planting scheme. Translucent highlights in the dark, glossy leaves of *Heuchera micrantha* 'Palace Purple' reflect the subtle colouring of *Cheiranthus mutabilis* in a glowing harmony. This partnership is woven around the light green, elegantly pointed foliage of *Alangium platanifolium*, which emphasizes the similar elegance of the heuchera leaf.

LEFT Foliage can enhance the effect of flowers in a variety of ways. On a small scale the flat rosettes of the purple plantain's deeply ribbed broad leaves physically and visually support the frail stems and pert flowers of bicoloured violas.

Grey and silver foliage

The most characteristic silvers are those finely dissected plants covered in woolly hairs: *Senecio bicolor cineraria* and the artemisias, *A. arborescens* at 1m/3ft plus, 'Powis Castle', one of the hardiest, growing to 60cm/24in, *A. stelleriana, A. splendens* and the low, spreading *A. schmidtiana* among them. *Anthemis cupaniana* is similar in texture but has the bonus of large white daisies freely produced on the wide-spreading plants in late spring, coinciding beautifully with white tulips, and often in summer if the plants are cut back almost to the ground after the first flowering. *Euryops acraeus* has small, entire leaves giving a more solid effect, and deep yellow flowers. *Helichrysum splendidum* has flowers of a similar colour but they are paler and less attractive and are best removed. Its leaves, however, maintain their silver elegance throughout the winter while other silvers look distinctly bedraggled. The tender *H. petiolare* and very small-leaved *H. microphyllum* (syn. *Pleco-stachys serpyllifolia*) also have leaves of a similar fine texture but on wide-spreading plants – ideal for intermingling among pale roses or for planting to trail over the edges of pots and hanging baskets. *Convolvulus althaeoides,* with deeply cut silvery leaves, will also trail but looks better climbing into low shrubs. It is perfect rambling through a lavender hedge.

Stachys lanata, with its much larger thick, felted leaves, is an excellent ground cover, reliably perennial but needing division from time to time to keep the flat mats of leafage looking fresh. Many people advise the nonflowering strain but I rather like the repeated verticals of its many dusky-pink and very woolly flower stems. They should, though, be removed after flowering as they then become scruffy. *Lychnis coronaria* is of similar stature but silkier and spreads by seed rather than vegetatively. The flower

The grey foliage of stachys, santolina and southernwood mingles with white roses to create an effect of ethereal delicacy. The edging of grey stone allows the stachys to spill out of the border, while separating its soft grey foliage from the yellow-green grass that could otherwise strike a discordant note.

Adding yellow to a grey and white planting results in a spring-like freshness of colouring. The pale yellow flowers of *Achillea* 'Moonshine', over their own neatly toothed grey leaves, associate delightfully with the silver filigree of *Artemisia* 'Powis Castle' and a soft grey edging of *Cerastium tomentosum*. The chalk-white cerastium flowers insinuate themselves among the artemisia, their translucent veins echoing the silver highlights on the artemisia leaves.

is a remarkable strong magenta in the species, good among old roses, foxgloves and many geraniums, but there is also a pale pink variety and a most beautiful pure white which comes true from seed if grown in isolation. Among the taller silvers, *Cytisus battandieri* and *Pyrus salicifolia* 'Pendula' are supreme but another useful background plant is *Salix elaeagnos,* a shrubby willow with small almost white leaves looking like a huge grey rosemary. Lower-growing silvers include *Salix lanata,* the santolinas and the many forms of lavender, the whitest being *Lavandula lanata,* not particularly hardy but easily grown from seed. Lastly, mention must be made of *Anaphalis nubigena,* a herbaceous perennial that dies away completely in the winter but reappears in spring with a flat dome of grey leaves looking just like a ghostly, diminutive *Viburnum davidii.* In late summer and autumn the anaphalis is covered in stiff, papery white

everlasting flowers, a marvellous companion for the autumn sedums, *Ceratostigma willmottianum* and *Nerine bowdenii.*

Many other grey-leaved plants derive their colouring from a wax coating on the leaves, imparting a smooth, glaucous sheen. *Convolvulus cneorum* must be the most brilliant of the silvers, looking as though it has just been dipped in aluminium paint and covered, in summer, with delightful pink-white bindweed funnels – but entirely noninvasive! *Crambe maritima,* many dianthus, *Eryngium maritimum* and *Hosta sieboldii* are all distinctly grey, as are the pink-flowered *Dicentra eximia* 'Boothman's Variety' and the pearly white *D. formosa oregana* 'Alba', and what a variety of leaf shapes and sizes these six plants encompass. Romneya, *Macleaya microcarpa* 'Coral Plume' and *Baptisia australis* are taller herbaceous perennials and where more permanence is required the fine-textured dome of *Coronilla glauca* is ideal, covered in fragrant yellow pea-flowers in spring and often again quite late in the autumn. Larger still are the various hardy eucalpytus and the tender but quick-growing *Eucalyptus globulus.*

Equally useful for their soft colouring are the innumerable grey-green leafed plants: *Achillea* 'Moonshine', *Geranium renardii, Veronica spicata incana,* helianthemums, phlomis, caryopteris, perovskia, buddlejas, cistus, tree peonies, valerian and many more. Special mention must be made of the shrubby *Abutilon vitifolium,* the herbaceous *Paeonia mlokosewitschii* and *Lysimachia ephemerum* and the many ground-covering epimediums for their particular beauty in flower as well as leaf. A flower garden that includes such plants will seldom lack beauty.

Flowers are not an outstanding characteristic of most conifers but some of the grey-leaved conifers are useful for their fine-textured foil and firm silhouettes to offset the ephemerality of flowers. The 'blue' forms of Lawson cypress (*Chamaecyparis lawsoniana*) such as 'Pembury Blue', 'Triomf van Boskoop' and the smaller 'Ellwoodii' or 'Fletcheri' usually come to mind, with *Chamaecyparis pisifera* 'Boulevard' providing a softer form. Increasingly popular are the grey-leaved junipers, from the widespreading *J. virginiana* 'Grey Owl' to the narrowly upright *J. scopulorum* 'Skyrocket' and the almost unreal blue of many varieties of *J. squamata.* One of the loveliest conifers is the fine-needled mound of *Pinus strobus* 'Nana', a dense teddy bear of a plant. None of the conifers will tolerate close smothering by climbers and other aggressive neighbours in a tapestry planting. Anything more than the light trails of *Clematis viticella* or a carefully controlled *Eccremocarpus scaber* will cause shaded branches to die out spoiling the winter outline of the conifer, one of its chief assets.

Useful as they undoubtedly are for their stability in larger schemes, conifers do not respond well to pruning. It is wiser to rely on rosemary, perovskia, lavender and other easily-pruned grey-leaved shrubs to achieve similar effects in small gardens.

Variegated and yellow foliage

The pale patches on variegated leaves are often susceptible to scorch if the leaves are subjected to water stress so the plants are better suited to shady positions. Out of direct sunlight the variegations are not only protected but often show up more conspicuously. Many yellow-leaved plants are also better in shade, providing a ray of sunshine to supplement the few flowers that grow well in shady parts of the garden.

Arum italicum var. *pictum* is remarkable in that its yellow-splashed glossy green leaves appear in the winter, lighting up dark corners and providing an ideal partner for snowdrops, winter aconites and early daffodils. To follow the arum there is nothing better than *Valeriana phu* 'Aurea', a herbaceous perennial that overwinters as a low, inconspicuous rosette but slowly expands in spring with the most brilliant yellow young foliage, slowly fading to green as summer advances and the spikes of small white flowers extend. It is a perfect companion for daffodils and forsythia and a brilliant contrast to blue scillas, chionodoxas, brunnera and forget-me-nots, but should be kept well away from the warmer tints of early tulips or yellow and white crocus.

Later in the season this golden effect can be continued using carpets of *Veronica prostrata* 'Trehane' (with its own spikes of bright blue flowers for contrast), clumps of golden meadowsweet (*Filipendula ulmaria aurea*) and the invaluable golden hop that scrambles over trellis, poles or supporting shrubs with splendid effect.

Golden-leaved shrubs, too, are useful for their glowing contribution, although the pink-flowered ones, such as *Ribes sanguineum* 'Brocklebankii' and *Weigela* 'Looymansii Aurea' are better out of flower. The same is not true of *Philadelphus coronarius* 'Aureus' or the new *Choisya ternata* 'Sundance', with scented white flowers, or of *Hypericum* 'Ysella' with yellow flowers to match its leaves.

Many evergreens have golden-leaved and golden- or white-variegated forms. Yew, privet, ivies, hollies, elaeagnus, euonymus and others are useful for

Variegated foliage can be used to effect in the flower garden. Here, bold white-margined leaves of *Brunnera macrophylla* 'Variegata' provide the brightest point of colour among soft violas, *Allium christophii*, *Hebe macrantha* and *Lithospermum purpureo-* *caeruleum*, but the leaves are beginning to show the scorched edges that are caused by lack of moisture. The clean white stripes of *Iris pallida* 'Argentea Variegata' in the background provide more reliable variegation in dry soils.

adding colour to the winter garden as well as for supporting the flower garden in many different ways. *Daphne odora* 'Aureo-marginata', with its scented purple flowers in early spring, is particularly useful in smaller gardens, where its cream-margined leaves will illuminate a semi-shaded spot and associate well with *Digitalis ambigua*, the pale epimediums and black-leaved ophiopogon. This lovely daphne will

also grow in full sun, where the variegation takes on a softer, almost glaucous tone.

Among smaller variegated plants, variegated honesty (*Lunaria annua*) is particularly useful for its tolerance of dry, shady corners where its white-splashed leaves show up well. The white flowered form is even more useful in shade than the normal dusky pink, and will come true from seed if other varieties are kept well away. *Hosta fortunei* 'Albopicta' is more subtle in colouring. Its young leaves unfold in spring as a uniform pale buttery yellow but expand to soft green with a broad yellow central zone, a perfect accompaniment for the mauve flower spikes in late summer. It will survive on quite dry soils and in sun as well as shade so is as versatile as it is beautiful. There are hundreds of other hostas, of course, with grey-blue, green or variegated leaves, and most are useful for associating with other flowers as well as producing their own.

Lamium maculatum, especially the white flowered and markedly white variegated forms, are also versatile, forming neat blankets of ground cover that insert themselves under taller plants without harm, creating many attractive associations of leaf and flower. *Cyclamen neapolitanum*, the delightful and completely hardy miniature cyclamen, produces its marbled leaves in late autumn, usually just after the flowers start to appear, but they persist throughout the winter, spring and early summer. Their ability to tolerate dry shade makes them invaluable – especially in the small garden – for extending the flower border into otherwise impossible gloom.

Not all variegated plants need, or even tolerate, shade. Many of the evergreen shrubs, especially, grow equally well and produce brighter yellow leaves in full sun. The same is true of *Robinia pseudoacacia* 'Frisia' and, to a lesser extent, *Gleditsia triacanthos* 'Sunburst', two trees that have become hackneyed by overuse in association with blue conifers or purple-leaved shrubs. Nevertheless, they are ideal as trees or stooled shrubs for creating a golden glow in the background of yellow, blue and white parts of the flower garden. *Cornus alba* 'Aurea', 'Spaethii' (yellow variegated), and 'Elegantissima' (white variegated) are also useful. The last-named has leaves that turn to apricot in autumn before falling to reveal the deep red stems that set off hellebores and other winter flowers to perfection. The cornus can also be left to grow into large mounds or pruned severely to fit into the smallest garden. Among herbaceous plants, *Phlox paniculata* 'Norah Leigh' and the stronger-growing but less strikingly variegated 'Harlequin' are so brightly marked with creamy white that they form focal points in the flower border long before their scented, pale lilac flowers are produced in mid-summer.

Spiraea japonica 'Goldflame' has leaves suffused with yellow, orange and pink when they emerge in spring, fading to yellow-green later in the summer. The dead-pink flowers are not a good accompaniment and are best removed (with the added advantage that hard pruning often encourages a second crop of young leaves), but the foliage glows with rich colouring and can be teamed up with many of the orange and warm yellow flowers of spring and early summer.

The golden elder, *Sambucus racemosa* 'Plumosa Aurea', is similar to the spiraea in its overall colouring but on a very different scale. Its deeply cut golden leaves arch on vigorous elder stems, reaching 2-3m/7-10ft on good soil in a single season, and take on warm reddish tints in the summer. If the plant is cut to ground level each year, the leaves will be largest and finest but if the one-year-old stems are left, thinning only the older and weaker stems, the elder will flower in spring and produce quantities of bright red fruits all along the branches in autumn.

At the other end of the spectrum from this bold spectacle, *Fuchsia magellanica* 'Versicolor' is the epitome of subtle beauty. Its slender, arching branches carry narrow leaves with irregular patches of pale green, cream and pink suffused beneath a pink-grey bloom. The flowers, with red sepals and deep purple skirts typical of the fuchsias, match the leaves in colouring and grace so the whole plant is a picture of slender charm.

FOCAL PLANTS

As well as having a background the flower garden needs focal points that draw the eye to the centre of the composition and emphasize its character. There may be a series of focal points. The eye will wander from the major focus to lesser ones and then perhaps on to other major points as one moves into other compartments of the garden. It is important to organize focal points so that the eyes, and perhaps the feet, are led easily from one to the other with no confusion or competition between them. It is also important that the focal point bears some relation to the scene of which it forms a part. Statuary, seats or buildings, or perhaps a fine, carefully framed view may provide focal points but in a flower garden it makes sense to use mainly plants.

To stand out in a garden picture, a plant must be remarkable in form, colour and/or texture, but if it differs markedly from its surroundings in all three features, it will be out of place. Where a plant serves as a focal point in the garden, one major attribute or, where a particularly striking effect is necessary, two should be emphasized. But there should always be some element of harmony.

Form, the overall shape and direction of growth of the plant, is its most durable characteristic. Plants such as weeping silver-leaved pear or an upright grey

RIGHT The clipped buttresses of the hedge flanking the path help to draw the eye, through the billowing forms of flower borders on either side, to the slender statue that forms the permanent focal point of this garden axis.

LEFT Spires of bright delphiniums, caught in the rays of the sun, temporarily create a dramatic focal point in the border. Purple salvias, expanding spikes of verbascums and distant blue delphiniums provide lesser points of emphasis, while sombre columns of clipped yew, not immediately obvious among the brighter flowers, echo the vertical accents.

juniper will stand out from a background of similarly soft-coloured and fine-textured but rounded plants. In a stronger coloured scheme, the pretty, weeping crab apple *Malus* 'Red Jade' or the fastigiate Irish yew might serve the same purpose. Plants with strongly vertical leaves or with an upward growth pattern such as yucca, *Dierama pulcherrimum* and many of the grasses also provide useful focal points, the effects varying from the low tufts of *Molinia caerulea* 'Variegata' to the great fountains of pampas, *Miscanthus sacchariflorus* or *Stipa gigantea*. Among the flowers, too, there are outstanding forms, the upright spires of delphinium and hollyhock or the weeping tassels of *Amaranthus caudatus,* which can be used as temporary focal points.

Texture, the size and boldness of the leaves and flowers, is a less durable characteristic of most plants, but a useful attribute. Usually one thinks in terms of coarse-textured plants as focal points: bergenia, acanthus, canna or catalpa for example, but fine-textured plants can also be remarkably different from their neighbours. Mounds of gypsophila, the finely cut leaves of *Coreopsis verticillata, Nigella damascena* or the clouds of London pride can stand out by their very indistinctness. Sometimes a plant combines boldness of leaf with airy flowers and such plants are particularly useful for adding emphasis in the flower garden. *Crambe cordifolia* is perhaps the most remarkable example of this, but the pale lavender *Limonium latifolium* has the same effect on a more modest scale.

Colour is usually the most ephemeral quality of a plant, unless that colour is possessed by the foliage, but contrast of colour is an extremely useful way of creating a temporary focal point in the flower garden, where its ephemerality is part of its charm. Whereas one might tire of a clever juxtaposition of upright and

The striking silhouette of the giant thistle, *Onopordum acanthium*, makes an increasingly spectacular focal point as its branching candelabrum of flowers reaches skywards. Its soft silver-grey colouring harmonizes with poppies, iris and centranthus. Stiff iris leaves and the arching flower heads of grey-leaved grass, *Helictotrichon sempervirens*, complete the picture.

horizontal conifers, the combination of delphinium spires with the flat plates of achillea, or heavy, arching peony blossoms with the shafts of blue iris will be gone before they have a chance to pall.

The plants with the brightest or whitest flowers in the most concentrated mass are most successful as focal points. *Lavatera* 'Mont Blanc' stands out from gypsophila of the same whiteness, delphiniums lord it over *Anchusa italica* or *Salvia patens,* and the torchlike kniphofias put geums and even day-lilies into the shade.

It is important not to introduce too many focal plants. A single group of crimson dahlias in a red border will provide a point of emphasis. Several groups will dilute the effect and a mass planting of dahlias needs to be relieved by fine-textured plants.

PLANNING THE FLOWER GARDEN

Defining the process of garden planning is rather like trying to unravel a spider's web: the evolution of a plan demands that all factors are taken into account together. The garden should have a prevailing sense of harmony with sufficient contrast to prevent that harmony becoming stultifying. It should have enough structure to set the flowers into context, to frame them and accentuate their colours. This back-bone should also create a comfortable degree of enclosure. The garden should be a beautiful place rather than just an interesting plant collection, although design and plant collection are by no means incompatible.

A garden of individual character will evolve by exploiting variations in the site, perhaps changes in level, certainly variations in aspect and outlook, and by limiting the planting to species that will flourish in the particular soil and situation of the garden.

The materials of the house, its age and plan, and the relationship between the principal rooms and the garden will all help to suggest an appropriate treatment for the flower garden.

Individuality will also emerge from the personalities of those involved in the making of the garden.

Some people will revel in bold, geometric shapes filled with bright colour; others will prefer the quieter charms of a wild flower meadow. Some will wish to potter all the hours of the day to perfect their private paradise; others will wish to collapse in it with the least possible effort. There is no right or wrong in these extremes.

The small garden

In a small garden, where everything is visible all the year round, each plant has to be attractive for as long as possible and, ideally, no plant should ever be positively unsightly. To a degree it is preferable, in a small garden, to have plants that are mildly attractive throughout the year than those whose beauty is outstanding but shortlived. This axiom has been taken to heart by many professional garden designers for whom such plants as *Viburnum davidii, Bergenia cordifolia, Cotoneaster dammeri* and *Mahonia japonica,* excellent plants in their own right, have provided the means of creating numerous foolproof but stereotyped gardens for their clients.

For the more interested garden owner, the fact that the garden is so small usually means that one can use annuals, tender perennials and other long-flowering plants without too great an expenditure in money or maintenance time, and it is often possible to indulge in complicated mixtures of plants that would be hopelessly difficult to maintain on a larger scale. There is scope, too, for gardening in containers. Window boxes and pots, however, require checking and probably watering every day, sometimes more than once a day in high summer, and unless one is prepared for this, and able to organize plantsitters during absences on holidays for example, it is pointless to begin with such features.

Another characteristic of many small gardens is that, because they are wholly enclosed on one side, by the house, and often on others by fences or walls, the creation of seclusion and the definition of space is not a problem. Indeed the degree of enclosure may be too great. Clothing the walls and fences with climbing plants creates the structure of the garden,

leaving nearly all the ground available for purely decorative planting, whereas in a large garden much of the ground area is occupied by structural planting.

In an enclosed garden, especially if it is shaded or heavily used, maintaining a patch of lawn is an onerous task and any imperfections will be conspicuous because of its small size. If the whole garden is paved there will be unlimited opportunities for plants to spill over and to occupy small gaps in the paving, resulting in a softer and more relaxed character than a

This small enclosed garden has benefitted from careful planning. The simple, uncluttered lawn is edged on one side by a path that curves gracefully into the mysterious shadows of overhanging pines, a perfect backdrop for flowers. The path allows plants to soften the border edge, while

in the foreground pots are clustered informally to blur the boundary between border and paving, with a trailing group of pale petunias, fuchsias and silvery *Helichrysum petiolare* strategically placed to interrupt the view of the lawn without interfering with mowing.

A SMALL ALL-YEAR GARDEN

Measuring only 5m/16ft square this garden has many advantages to offset its limited size.

It is situated on a warm steeply sloping site, that, although surrounded by other houses, commands attractive distant views between the chimney pots of houses below. The garden is terraced with a retaining wall and steep steps of rough grey stone separating the upper part, barely 2m/7ft deep, from a secluded lower garden 3m/10ft across. In a garden of this size every plant clearly needs to earn its keep for as much of the year as possible.

A trellis enclosing one corner is clad with *Clematis cirrhosa balearica* for its evergreen foliage and winter flowers, with *Eccremocarpus scaber* in its soft yellow form, hardy and nearly evergreen in the mild climate, for summer. Softening the hard outline of the trellis is a single plant of *Cornus alba* 'Elegantissima', hard-pruned to produce large variegated leaves and the brightest red young stems, and at the base of the screen the dark leaves and cascading purple flower sprays of *Hebe hulkeana* team with the much finer textured foliage of its late-summer flowering relative *Parahebe catarractae*. Against this dark base, still bearing a scattering of purple flowers, the clear pink flowers of *Nerine bowdenii* emerge in the autumn and last well into early winter in most years. On the house wall, also of grey stone, the tiny dark green leaves of *Azara microphylla* show up well, bearing quantities of equally tiny vanilla-scented flowers in late winter. It shares the wall with *Jasminum officinale* for summer scent, kept in place by rigorous pruning, and *Clematis viticella,* allowed to wander at will through the jasmine and azara.

In front of the simple metal railing that tops the retaining wall are two shrubs: *Hypericum* 'Hidcote' on one side merging into the cornus with its grey-green leaves and deep yellow flowers, and on the other side, separated from the hypericum to frame a view of distant hills, a deep blue hydrangea. Below them are two hostas, a small group of pulmonarias and a patch of *Stachys lanata,* similar in leaf shape, very different in size but associating well with their varied grey and variegated leaves, and providing some flower from early spring to autumn. Large- and small-leaved variegated ivies and the common periwinkle peep out here and there from among the other plants, spilling over the path and, in the case of the smaller ivy, climbing up to vie with the yellow of the hypericum flowers. These three evergreens are particularly valuable in winter when the hostas have gone, their place taken by a patch of snowdrops. Set into this backbone of permanent plants is a changeable array of simple terracotta pots filled with annuals in summer and fragrant wallflowers for spring. The path near the top of the steps is nearly blocked by the large, glaucous rosettes of *Beschorneria yuccoides,* dramatic enough in leaf but quite amazing in those summers when it decides to produce a flower spike or two, arching bright crimson-pink stems clad with pink and green bells and crimson bracts to a height of 2m/7ft or more.

At one end of the narrow upper garden, steep steps descend between a large bay (*Laurus nobilis*) and a garrya-covered fence screening the neighbour's garden. Above the garrya grows one of two trees in the garden, *Prunus subhirtella* 'Autumnalis', with a sprinkling of pale pink flowers from late autumn until spring. Below it the plants are mainly dark evergreens, bergenia, skimmia, sarcococca and *Viburnum davidii* to simulate the shady recesses of an extensive woodland. A golden hop (*Humulus japonicus* 'Aureus') climbs through the garrya in summer, creating its own shade, and odd plants of white foxglove, lilies and tulips light up the 'woodland' gloom.

On the other side of the steps, the treatment is in total contrast. The bay tree arises out of purple-leaved *Berberis thunbergii atropurpurea* and bergenias to balance the darker planting, but the berberis merges into the bright pink splashes on the leaves of *B.* 'Rose Glow' and thence into a tapestry of hardy fuchsias, penstemons of pink and magenta, grey-leaved rue (its yellow flowers rigorously removed), lavender, rosemary and *Artemisia* 'Powis Castle', topped by the smoky grey-pink leaves of *Fuchsia magellanica* 'Versicolor'. Stout clumps of hardy, deep blue agapanthus, trails of *Convolvulus althaeoides* with its finely cut silver leaves and clear pink funnels, and cloudy tufts of the glaucous *Origanum laevigatum,* which has minute, darker pink flowers above aromatic foliage in the autumn, complete a picture of soft colour and luxuriant growth.

The narrow path curves round the bay tree into the most sheltered part of the garden, in a corner of the retaining wall. The grey stone is nearly covered in the pink-splashed leaves of *Actinidia kolomikta* above the glossy leaves and pink tubular flowers of *Abelia × grandiflora*. A seat in the corner is surrounded by mounds of various softly-coloured herbs growing in gaps in the paving, and a simple arbour over the seat, connecting with the railing above, is partially covered in white-flowered runner beans. Dappled shade from the hottest midday sun is provided by *Acacia dealbata;* this plant will soon outgrow its position but, in the meantime, holds its fine grey foliage over the lower garden in summer and produces fluffy yellow 'mimosa' balls that can be seen from the upper garden in winter. Pots in the lower garden are fewer but larger, partly because carrying water down the steps each day is arduous, although the grey-leaved *Argyranthemum frutescens*, salmon pink variegated zonal pelargonium 'Chelsea Gem', blue *Convolvulus mauritanicus* and silver-leaved helichrysums will often survive for days without watering.

This is not the entire planting of the garden of course. Any spaces that would be bare in winter are quickly filled with bulbs, and small plants are tucked into every space between and beneath the shrubs. The bright colours of the upper garden, the cool green and white of the miniscule 'woodland garden' and the soft luxuriance of the lower 'Mediterranean' garden, each with its carefully disciplined but interrelated colour scheme, create interest out of all proportion to this garden's minute size.

1   *Beschorneria yuccoides*   A
2   *Jasminum officinale*   S
3   *Clematis viticella*   A
4   *Parahebe catarractae*   S
5   *Azara microphylla*   W
6   *Nerine bowdenii*   A
7   *Hebe hulkeana*
8   *Clematis cirrhosa balearica*   W
9   *Eccremocarpus scaber*   S/A
10   Hostas   A
11   *Pulmonaria saccharata*   Sp
12   *Hydrangea hortensia*   S/A
13   Periwinkle and variegated ivy
14   *Stachys lanata*   S
15   *Hypericum* 'Hidcote'   S/A
16   *Cornus alba* 'Elegantissima'
17   *Laurus nobilis* (bay)
18   *Actinidia kolomikta*
19   *Abelia × grandiflora*   A
20   *Acacia dealbata*   W
21   *Bergenia cordifolia*   W
22   *Berberis thunbergii atropurpurea*
23   *Origanum laevigatum*
24   Hardy fuchsias   S/A
25   Rosemary   S
26   *Penstemon heterophyllus*,
     P. 'Evelyn' and
     P. 'Garnet'   S
27   Rue
28   *Convolvulus althaeoides*
29   Runner beans (white-
     flowered)   S/A
30   Herbs
31   Lavender   S
32   *Artemisia* 'Powis Castle'
33   Agapanthus   A
34   *Berberis* 'Rose Glow'
35   *Fuchsia magellanica*
     'Versicolor'   S/A
36   *Viburnum davidii*   Sp
37   *Skimmia japonica*   Sp
38   White flowers (foxgloves,
     lilies and tulips)   Sp
39   *Sarcococca hookeriana*
     digyna   W
40   *Prunus subhirtella*
     'Autumnalis'   W
41   *Humulus japonicus* 'Aureus'
     (hop)
42   *Garrya elliptica*   W
P   Pots with varied planting

Sp=spring
S=summer
A=autumn
W=winter

garden designed around a small lawn. With the ground plane largely covered by carpeting plants and the area available for gardening on walls, in window boxes and other containers often exceeding the ground space, it is not difficult to transform a dingy back yard into an oasis of colour and fragrance.

A problem that often arises in small gardens is that the enclosure is too obvious; the effect is claustrophobic and often dark. Covering parts of the walls with loose-growing climbers does much to relieve this and softens the line. Strangely, it also alleviates the

darkness of a shady garden: the plants create a mosaic of black shadows and relatively light greens instead of the uniform gloom of shaded walls.

Often the enclosure is not only obtrusive but unpleasantly rigid: a flat, square garden surrounded by vertical walls has an oppressively boxlike character. Here there is also scope for breaking up the rectangularity by sinking or raising parts of the garden, incorporating low walls, steps, raised beds and sunken areas to add interest.

In a moderately small garden there may be room for a loggia or pergola along one side of the garden. Even a single pillar, perhaps connected to the house or garden wall with overhead beams to frame the sky, will form an arch from some points of view, a picture frame or loggia from others and, suitably clothed with climbing plants, will obscure the continuity of surrounding walls.

Occasionally it is possible to reduce the solidity of the enclosure with honeycomb brickwork, wrought-iron grills, trellis or decorative concrete blocks. Where an opening in the wall is not feasible, it is quite easy to create the effect of one by using a mirror. At first glance, light reflected from within the garden looks exactly like a hole in the wall with a glimpse into the next garden. Great care is needed in siting the mirror, though, to avoid reflecting the observer as much as possible. Placing a mirror squarely across the main vista in the garden, for example, will give you mainly a view of you advancing on yourself, which can be very disconcerting. Placing the mirror at a 45 degree angle to a path will reflect what is at right angles to the viewer, extending the apparent length of the vista. By siting the mirror only a few degrees off square, it is possible to create a vista 'out' to a focal point actually next to the observer. A mirror opposite a window, for instance, could reflect a pot of flowers and 'place' it at the end of a view through the garden wall and into another garden!

The use of mirrors in a garden may sound gimmicky but, in moderation, it is an effective technique for increasing the apparent extent of the garden while doubling the value derived from

RIGHT In a large garden, concentration of detail near the house and reliance on simple shrub and tree masses for the background enhance the sense of space and greatly reduce maintenance. In this example, the brick path creates intricacy of scale and allows every charming incident within the flower border to take its rightful place in the scheme, while a broad sweep of lawn leads the eye out into the wider landscape.

LEFT One or two carefully sited pillars, connected to the house or garden wall by overhead beams, can relieve the severity of a boxlike enclosure, while providing additional space for the introduction of flowers climbing up and over the supports.

flowers and foliage reflected in it.

Dealing with a boxlike garden can be challenging, but a worse problem arises in exposed small gardens bounded only by a few strands of wire. This can be solved with a free-standing, light trellis screen, covered with annual climbers for almost instant effect, and incorporating one or more perennial climbers for lasting protection.

It is seldom a good idea to surround the whole garden as this will create just the unpleasant boxlike enclosure that many gardeners struggle to disguise. If gaps are left for the eye to wander out of the garden it will create a greater sense of space and distance.

Whether one is trying to reduce the effect of excessive enclosure in the garden or to build up a structure where the enclosure is inadequate, the aim should be to create an interesting and harmonious three-dimensional 'container' that can be clothed and decorated with flowering plants.

The large garden

Most of the beauty of a large garden must rely on breadth and simplicity of effect. For human comfort it is important to plan a small-scale garden within a large one and there is scope for attractive incidents along well-used paths and in other important parts of the garden. However, maintenance is an ever-present concern and should be minimized by concentrating intricate details into a small area and relying on breadth of effect in the rest of the garden.

Size can be exploited by the use of flowering trees and bold sweeps of shrub borders. Large groups of trouble-free herbaceous perennials in the foreground set off by broad expanses of lawn, much of it converted to a mosaic of bulbs and other simple flowers in meadow communities, will enhance the effect. For more adventurous gardeners, borders of mixed annuals or even larger 'cornfields' of annual flowers could provide the brilliant finishing touch.

THE GRAND SCALE

Although this is the age of the small garden, not everyone's plot is a pocket handkerchief, and this border scheme will be of use to anyone planning or replanning a large flower garden. At the same time it will also emphasize that the planning principles are the same as for a small border.

The largest border I have planned was over 100m/360ft long and 6m/20ft wide over much of that length, widening to double that at one end, where it curved round to meet the blank wall of a garden pavilion. It was backed by a honey-coloured stone wall, varying in height, and edged by a wide gravel path of the same colour separating the border from expansive lawns. The soil was light and the situation hot, receiving the midday sun, but decades of cultivation and the promise of more to come meant that it was possible to include plants that required substantially higher fertility than the native soil could offer.

The main stipulations were that the border should require *relatively* little labour for a herbaceous border (not too many annuals or too much staking), that it should be at its best in high summer and, surprisingly difficult, that it should be a border of mixed colours, not colour-graded. Where to start?

Firstly the setting. The width, although substantial, was not very great for a border of such length. Fortunately the high wall meant that climbers could be used to provide the height necessary for the scheme without taking too much of the border's width, and having a path of generous proportions in the foreground meant that edging plants could stray forward on to the path, bringing it into the composition and accentuating the apparent width of the border. Even so, it was important to break up the

length of the border with occasional groups of high plants, chosen for flower and foliage, to create a series of alcoves so that the border was gradually revealed as one walked along the path. The border was visible from several hundred metres/yards and so it was vital that it should look good from a distance.

There were four key points along the border, described here starting from the narrower end (to the right of the small plan), which received the morning sun. The path emerged from dark evergreens to reveal the whole border. Near the middle, gate piers marked the entrance to the walled gardens and flanked a double border that had been planted with a clearly defined colour scheme: deep reds and oranges fading to yellows, lavender, purple, pink and finally white by the gate. A second gate opened on to a small enclosure planted with flowers of apricot with lavender accents. The border ended at the blank wall of the garden pavilion (left on the plan). The path continued into a quiet woodland garden.

The policy for planting the border evolved from all these points taken together. Climbers would be used to adorn, but not entirely conceal, the wall. Occasional groups of shrubs, supplemented in season by tall herbaceous perennials, would divide the border into a series of irregular bays of various sizes. Edging plants would be chosen to extend over the path and to create a well-furnished outline throughout the summer. In particular, the intermediate bearded iris, which had been a considerable feature of the garden in the past, but which left a very ragged edge to the border by high summer, would be moved back a rank, behind ground-covering perennials. Light evergreens would enclose the

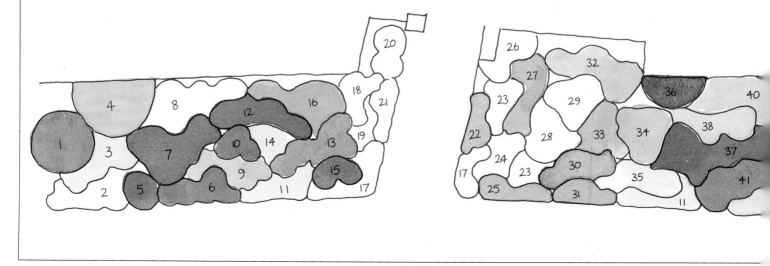

narrower end of the border to link it with tall yews and hollies beyond the path, white flowers and grey foliage would flank the middle gateway, effectively extending the colour-graded border within the walled garden (as it was rather short for its purpose), and the second opening in the wall would have a concentration of mauve and purple flowers to echo the minor colour within the enclosed garden. At the other end of the border, the rather dark effect of high walls largely in shade with the woodland beyond would be accentuated by using purple foliage, tall enough in places to break the stark outline of the otherwise attractive pavilion, interlaced with white and other pale flowers to both intensify and lighten the shade. To enhance the distant view of the border it was decided to concentrate the yellow and white flowers, the most conspicuous from a long way off, into substantial masses.

Having decided on this policy, the choice of plants became much easier. Lists for different months, different heights and different colours were extracted from a wide range of sources. At each of the key points in the border, plant groupings were carefully arranged for the desired effect, then the schemes were extended, separating bright yellows and oranges from pinks and purples with generous barriers of blue, lavender and white and indulging, from time to time, in harmonious groups of very similar colouring, but otherwise trying to maintain a mosaic of varying colour. As each mini-plan extended to meet its neighbour it was necessary to backtrack on occasions so that the boundaries would meet on friendly terms, until the separate parts of the border merged into a unified whole.

1	*Buddleja crispa*
2	*Physostegia virginiana* 'Summer Snow'
3	Antirrhinum (pale yellow)
4	*Cotinus coggygria*
5	*Dierama pulcherrimum*
6	*Salvia × superba* 'May Night'
7	Eremurus and fennel
8	*Althaea rosea* (white)
9	Intermediate bearded iris (chrome yellow)
10	*Crocosmia masonorum*
11	Potentilla (pale yellow)
12	*Salvia* 'Queen Victoria'
13	*Nepeta × faassenii*
14	*Anthemis tinctoria* 'E.C. Buxton'
15	*Kniphofia nelsonii*
16	*Salvia involucrata* 'Bethellii'
17	*Geranium sanguineum album*
18	*Anaphalis triplinervis*
19	Agapanthus (white)
20	*Romneya × hybrida*
21	Aquilegia (white)
22	*Eryngium bourgatii*
23	*Malva moschata alba*
24	Intermediate bearded iris (white)
25	*Penstemon heterophyllus*
26	*Eupatorium ligustrinum*
27	*Sidalcea* 'Sussex Beauty'
28	*Crambe cordifolia*
29	Dahlia (medium white)
30	*Linum perenne*

31	*Sedum* 'Vera Jameson'
32	*Macleaya microcarpa*
33	*Coreopsis verticillata*
34	*Kniphofia* 'Ada'
35	Intermediate bearded iris (pale yellow)
36	*Ceanothus* 'Autumnal Blue'
37	*Helenium* 'Coppelia'
38	*Solidago* 'Mimosa'
39	*Oenothera missouriensis*
40	*Rudbeckia maxima*
41	*Tradescantia × andersoniana* 'Isis'
42	*Hemerocallis* 'Burning Daylight'
43	*Geranium wallichianum* 'Buxton's Variety'
44	*Clematis recta* 'Purpurea'
45	*Althaea rosea* (crimson)
46	*Lonicera periclymenum* 'Serotina'
47	*Anchusa azurea*
48	*Potentilla* 'Gibson's Scarlet'
49	Dahlia (dwarf scarlet)
50	*Hemerocallis* 'Alan'
51	Dahlia (tall, dark, crimson)
52	*Polygonum amplexicaule*
53	*Sedum spectabile* 'Autumn Joy'
54	Aquilegia (pink)
55	Antirrhinum (pink)
56	*Echinacea purpurea*
57	*Aster × frikartii*
58	*Althaea rosea* (pink)
59	*Cotinus coggygria* 'Foliis Purpureis'

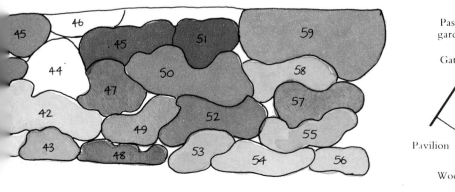

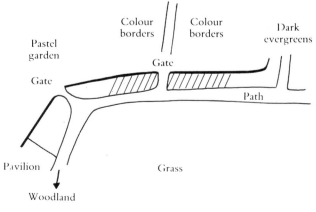

WAYS WITH FLOWERS

In choosing plants for the flower garden, the aim should be to create an overall sense of harmony in colour, texture and form, with a degree of contrast to provide relief. Contrast is frequently overemphasized in gardening literature: it is often forgotten that satisfying contrast cannot be achieved without harmony.

Harmony is created by gradual changes in colour and by repetition of plant forms and textures. It need not be confined to pastel schemes or to misty, fine-textured plants. A brilliant group of orange and mahogany French marigolds with dark-leaved cannas is harmonious in colour; a border of giant reeds, arching grasses, crocosmias, agapanthus and other narrow-leaved plants creates a striking harmony of form, very different in effect from the quieter harmony of soft pinks and mauves.

The effect of total harmony can be immensely satisfying but it will be fleeting, because the brain adjusts the messages it receives from the eyes to accord with preconceived views of a 'normal' world. If you stare hard at a bright green square of paper and then at a white wall, your brain will tell you that a square piece of the wall is red. In the same way, the first impression of an all-silver garden may be breathtaking but, after a few minutes, the brain will have 'adjusted' the grey leaves to green. The garden will then have much the same impact as an overexposed photograph. Harmony loses its point unless relieved by an element of contrast.

Of course there are varying degrees of contrast. Imagine the huge dark leaves and striking, upright form of the purple castor oil plant (*Ricinus communis* 'Gibsonii') growing through a carpet of small, feathery-leaved golden feverfew and the contrast is complete, whereas the grey swordlike leaves of *Iris pallida* piercing a carpet of catmint offer contrast of an altogether gentler kind.

Harmony and contrast also exist in the garden at a range of scales. They can coexist within a single flower. The clear blue and black markings within the flower of a gazania, for example, offer brilliant contrast to the orange and yellow rays of its petals. Wisteria, a marvel of colour harmony with its grey bark, grey-green leaves and soft grey-blue flowers, derives extra charm from the contrast of its straight, pendulous racemes of flowers with the tortuous sculpture of its stems.

On a larger scale, two or three plants may flower together to form a composition within a frame of greenery, harmonizing with each other but contrasting with the quieter background to make an incident in the garden. Incidents combine to create a border that contrasts with cool, green approaches or with the colours of adjacent borders.

By careful planning of harmonious plant associations, relieved by occasional and not too forceful contrasts, the flower garden will achieve a degree of variety that satisfies both the eye and the spirit.

A TIME FOR FLOWERS

To create a permanently satisfying garden picture, it is necessary to give some thought to the distribution of flowering plants throughout the garden at different seasons.

In winter and early spring, flowers are relatively few and often quite delicate, in appearance if not in constitution. If they are grouped near the house and

In the most satisfying garden pictures an overall harmony is relieved by an element of contrast. Here the vertical spires of blush white verbascums, pale pink linaria and deep blue *Salvia* × *superba* combine in gentle harmony; the rounded flower heads of valerian, on their straight, stiff stems harmonize in colour, but contrast in form.

LEFT A carpet of stitchwort (*Stellaria holostea*) and sharp yellow *Euphorbia cyparissias* beneath the flower-wreathed branches of a young *Malus floribunda* has all the freshness of spring. The effect is enhanced by the pale yellow-green new growth of laurels in the background and by the dark shadows of the large laurel leaves.

RIGHT The warm light of autumn is echoed in the dusky-red heads of *Sedum telephium* slowly fading to rusty brown as winter advances. The everlasting flowers of *Anaphalis triplinervis*, snow-white in late summer, also pick up autumn tints as they fade. Both plants attract crowds of butterflies to add to the colour of the autumn garden.

near frequently-used paths about the garden they can be appreciated at close range for their fragile beauty and for the exquisite fragrance that many possess. In the winter garden tiny incidents can often bring great delight: a single plant of the diminutive *Cyclamen coum*, a few *Iris reticulata* or a clump of snowdrops strategically placed will defy the dreariness of winter for many weeks.

Concentrating winter flowers near the house does not mean, of course, that this important part of the garden will be ugly for the rest of the year. Hellebores, sarcococcas, *Viburnum tinus* and *Garrya elliptica,* so useful in the winter garden, are evergreens that provide a good background to summer flowers. Witch hazels, *Viburnum × bodnantense,* winter sweet and the winter-flowering honeysuckles and jasmine are also attractive in their summer leaf. Winter-flowering bulbs such as snowdrops, aconites, the early *Scilla tubergeniana* (syn. *S. mischtschenkoana*) and early species of crocus, and the earliest herbaceous plants such as the lovely *Adonis amurensis* 'Fukujukai', die away soon after flowering so the space they occupy can provide a second season of interest. Many bulbs actually benefit from the drying out of the soil by summer-growing plants.

As spring arrives it is almost too easy to fill the garden with flowers. Flowering trees and shrubs, bulbs and early herbaceous plants create a dramatic spectacle among unfolding foliage of varying tints. The main tasks in grouping spring flowers are to avoid the worst colour-clashes – the acid yellow of early daffodils with egg-yolk crocuses or sharp yellow forsythia with pink cherries, for example – and to ensure that the abundance of blossom leaves room for the flowers at other times of the year. How many rock gardens, for instance, have anything to show after the aubrieta and golden alyssum have exchanged their flowers for mildewed leaves?

The superabundance of spring flowers does not lessen the pleasure to be gained from careful plant association. A garden that alternately exploits the delicacy of white spiraeas and yellow daffodils, forsythia or *Kerria japonica* and the brilliant colours of

tulips, polyanthus and oriental poppies will give infinitely more pleasure than one in which blotches of spring colour are scattered at random through the half-awakened garden.

In summer, warm weather invites exploration of the less accessible parts of larger gardens. Colour is abundant and varied among herbaceous plants, roses, shrubs and bedding plants.

Autumn offers its own diversity, from the soft colours of Michaelmas daisies, sedums, buddlejas,

A well-planned flower garden provides a shifting mosaic of colour as the seasons progress.

In spring (top), drifts of aquilegia and violas occupy the foreground, with the promise of flowers soon to unfold from fat iris buds towering up against the fresh foliage of other herbaceous plants.

In high summer (right) the border seems full of flowers: delphiniums, white and pink valerian, *Salvia* × *superba*, catmint and yellow day-lilies in broad drifts. The iris foliage in the foreground provides a foil, and closer inspection reveals many spaces among the flowers for later plants.

The warm light of autumn is complemented by the soft colours of asters, sedums and eupatorium and the starlike seed heads of *Echinops ritro*. In winter (above) the importance of backbone planting is revealed, with mounds of grey foliage, vertical straw-coloured grasses and swordlike iris leaves effective in frost, mist or snow.

caryopteris and *Perovskia atriplicifolia,* and mounds of grey foliage plants that have been accumulating all summer, to the harvest-festival richness of glowing dahlias, chrysanthemums and pre-frost summer bedding among the reds and golds of autumn foliage. In equal quantities, the misty blue-greys and brilliant orange-reds are not good neighbours, but a little of one will highlight the qualities of the other by dramatic contrast.

The way in which the plants are grouped together in each season affects the character of the garden. The various species may be mingled in a fine-textured tapestry, arranged in groups for pictorial effect, or planted in broad masses of one or two sorts only.

TAPESTRY PLANTING

Nineteenth-century gardeners devised (or perhaps revised, as the idea was common in late medieval gardens) a system of planting that they called 'promiscuous gardening', now more widely known by the less ambiguous term 'tapestry planting'. By 'promiscuous gardening' the Victorians meant the mixing together of many different flowers into a homogeneous blend. Each variety was repeated throughout the border and each plant was surrounded by plants of different varieties, producing an effect resembling a delicate tapestry, with many points of colour contributing to a general tone.

The inspiration for this tapestry planting can be seen in the species-rich meadows and cornfields of an era predating chemical weed control. The plant communities resulting from traditional agricultural practices have as much appeal today for their nostalgic interest as for the beautiful pictures they create.

Viewed at close range, there are often violent clashes of colour: scarlet poppies and purple corncockle, or the orange-yellow of bird's foot trefoil with pink clover. However, because the points of colour are so small in relation to the total scene, and because they are embedded in a soothing green background, any clashes only add vibrancy to the picture. At a greater distance they disappear as the softer colours recede into the background and the brighter colours predominate, giving an attractive sparkle to the meadow or cornfield.

Rich wild flower communities offer many subtle delights. From a short way off, only the taller flowers are visible: the field or meadow may seem full of cornflowers or buttercups. At closer range, looking down into the flowery carpet rather than across it, the monochromatic sheet of colour opens up: the cornflowers or buttercups disperse into irregularly scattered groups, revealing a multicoloured tapestry of other species beneath and between. The eye will select balanced compositions from the random array of this kaleidoscope, focusing on individual groups of a single species that form attractive constellations, on attractive harmonies among neighbouring plants, or on the occasional sharp contrast.

Usually the effects are appreciated subconsciously. It is rather like being carried along by a sweeping melody instead of registering individual notes. Sometimes the eye will rest longer on individual compositions, but even these vignettes of the whole will reveal compositions within the composition. The subtlety of the effects perceived is a major element of their enchantment. They are simultaneously stimulating and restful.

Subtlety of variation within a tapestry planting occurs in time as well as in space. As early flowers fade, their ripening seed heads disappear among the elongating stems of later species. There is no sudden, dramatic change, but colour and species composition evolve gradually through the growing season. In a natural community, the season of interest is relatively short and finely attuned to natural events. Species are orchestrated into a spring display by the need to ripen their seed before hay-making or to synchronize their growth and seeding with the corn. In other habitats, flowers may emerge simultaneously to exploit a brief rainy season or burst forth in a splendid autumn display after the fires created by summer thunderstorms. In the flower garden such seasonal limitations can be avoided and tapestry planting will provide a source of delight for many months.

A border of mixed annuals

The easiest way to create a tapestry effect is by sowing packets of mixed seeds of hardy annuals, whether native cornfield annuals, exotic species and cultivated varieties, or both. The season may start with multicoloured *Linaria maroccana*, slender *Viscaria oculata* and quick-growing California poppies, rise to a climax of cornflowers, Shirley poppies, gypsophila, clarkia and all the other trusty annuals and continue until the last *Salvia sclarea*, *Echium plantagineum* and *Lavatera trimestris* finally succumb to autumn rains and frost.

To start such a feature, prepare a fertile seedbed, firming and raking it to produce a good tilth, then leave it for 10 to 14 days for the weed seeds near the

The relationship between gardening and tapestry is evident in this finely stitched blend of herbaceous plants. Crimson roses, scarlet *Lychnis chalcedonica*, orange alstroemeria, yellow oenotheras and achilleas combine in a warm glow of colour made darker and richer by the bronze stems and leaves of purple orache.

surface to germinate. These can then be burned off chemically, using paraquat, or physically with a flame gun. Shallow hoeing, scraping the soft weeds off at ground level with a minimum of soil disturbance, is a reasonable though rather less satisfactory alternative for those who are anti-technology. Having eliminated the majority of weeds that are likely to germinate, sow the seed mixture in straight drills approximately 20cm/8in apart (35cm/15in if only tall

annuals are being sown). This method is preferable to broadcasting, as raking in broadcast seed disturbs the soil and brings weed seeds to the surface, where they will germinate.

Sowing in drills also makes it easy to thin out the seedlings after germination: just chop out sections of the row with a hoe to leave small clusters of seedlings at 20cm/8in spacings. During this thinning operation, any weed seedlings that have appeared should be removed. After that it should only be necessary to remove the odd large weed here and there. Smaller ones will be concealed by the dense growth of annuals and, once the annuals themselves have covered the ground, there will be little further opportunity for weed seeds to germinate.

During the summer, the delicate blend of colour will provide endless pleasure, growing in height and changing gradually in its composition as later-flowering annuals come into their own. As summer wanes, the mixture will gradually take on a more jaded appearance. Flowers will be dying faster than they can be replaced and the dried corpses of spent plants will become increasingly obvious. Heavy rain may cause the taller plants to collapse as they lose the support of their neighbours.

Just when the appearance becomes unacceptable depends on the weather (the plants fading faster in hot dry weather) and on the individual gardener. The more tidy-minded will consider the border finished by late summer, while others will keep the scheme into early autumn for the sake of the softer colours of the latest-flowering species and for the brightly coloured butterflies that feed on many of them. Where the mixed annual border is to be followed by wallflowers, pansies, polyanthus or other spring bedding plants the annuals should be pulled up by early autumn to prepare the ground for planting.

Cornfield annuals are one of the easiest and most charming ways to introduce colour into the flower garden. The mingled flowers of red flax and poppy, yellow corn marigold and annual chrysanthemum, soft pink viscaria and blue cornflowers create a succession of flower pictures as one species succeeds another.

Where spring flowers do not form part of the scheme and the border is not conspicuously placed, the annuals can be left until winter when the shrivelled remains will be easy to pull up for composting or burning.

After the first year, it is possible simply to allow those annuals which have seeded themselves to reappear, and then to chop through the carpet of seedlings with a hoe in two directions to leave small clumps of seedlings at intervals. However, the weed population will gradually increase year by year and, unless the border is left well into the autumn to complete the ripening of seed on late-flowering plants, the mixture will soon become dominated by early-flowering varieties so that the border is over by late summer.

Varying the mix

While sowing from packets of mixed seeds is a useful way to begin, as they often contain seed of little-known but interesting flowers, with a little experience it soon becomes possible to design a mix specifically to suit a particular situation. A mixture could be confined to low-growing varieties, for example, or to soft mauves and pinks or brilliant yellows and oranges. It might be advisable to concentrate on early-flowering varieties for a summer cottage, or on late-flowering annuals when the family are likely to be away from home for much of the summer, or there may be an interest in annuals that will sustain colourful butterflies.

It is easy to collect seed from most annuals by gathering the seed heads as they turn from green to yellow-brown, storing the heads in airy paper bags until quite dry, then crushing or shaking them as necessary to release the seeds. The seeds should be stored dry in a refrigerator until sown. They will not be as clean and free from debris as those obtained from professional seedsmen, nor will the varieties remain constant and uniform as they would under the careful selection and breeding procedures of the seedsman, but neither of these points is likely to be of any importance in a sowing of mixed annuals.

The place for mixed annuals

Beds and borders of mixed annuals are effective when seen from a distance, when the dominant components of the ever-changing scheme form broad sheets of colour, and at very close range so that one looks down into the lovely variety of flowers. Viewed from the middle distance a mixed annual border lacks breadth of effect and the generally fine texture of flowers and leaves creates an insubstantial, temporary appearance.

However, it is easy to achieve a degree of firmness in the middle distance. Take inspiration from medieval and early Renaissance knot gardens and enclose formal beds of mixed annuals within low perennial planting – dwarf box for the long term, London pride or thrift for a quicker effect. Again, bold-textured plants used as accents in the border will relieve the monotonously fine texture of most flowering annuals. *Ricinus communis, Eucalyptus globulus, Perilla nankinensis* and the many varieties of *Canna indica* with their bold green, bronze or striped leaves are obvious examples of suitable plants, but the stately white-flowered *Nicotiana sylvestris,* the green form of love-lies-bleeding (*Amaranthus caudatus*) or the green domes of *Kochia scoparia*, all half-hardy annuals, make excellent focal points in a sea of mixed annuals, where a less striking contrast is desirable.

Perennial promiscuity

Nineteenth-century gardeners usually used herbaceous perennials to create their promiscuous borders; a few such borders still exist and are delightful to look at, but they are difficult to manage. Neighbouring plants compete strongly with each other and, if left in position for several years, the most vigorous plants will soon crowd out less successful species.

Because of this, mixed perennial borders only work if the contents of the border are lifted and divided regularly; and digging up, dividing and replanting often deep-rooted perennials is much harder work than pulling up dead annuals and resowing the following spring. Furthermore, because each perennial will normally be larger and carry more flowers than the closely spaced annuals in a mixed border, the tapestry effect of the perennials is much coarser in texture and only really succeeds on a large scale.

The flowery mead

One way of achieving a low-maintenance tapestry border using perennials is to take a direct lesson from nature: to disperse the flowers among low-growing grasses and create a flowery mead. The tapestry remains, softened by the flowers of the grasses, but the chores of regular digging and dividing are avoided because plants are separated from each other and reduced in competitive vigour by the grass. Annual cutting down and clearing up of the border is replaced by mowing once or twice a year and collecting the hay.

In recent years there has been a considerable interest in wild flower meadows throughout the industrial world, for their own charm and because they attract butterflies, seed-eating finches and other attractive wildlife. In a garden setting, there is no reason to confine the meadow to native plants. Plants from similar climatic zones can be introduced into the meadow alongside the natives to create a 'wild garden' in the sense used by William Robinson and his contemporaries. European cranesbills, American lupins, Japanese anemones and the various species of campanula, centaurea and scabious from around the world could all find a place in the larger wild garden, growing in thin grassland. But although there is room for many hardy exotics in such a scheme, it is best to avoid the more highly bred varieties with large double flowers. Not only do they look out of place in a meadow setting but they are unlikely to survive the rigours of competition in the meadow.

The most satisfactory way I have found to create a meadow is to mow the grass very low in autumn and to plant vigorous young seedlings of the flowering plants into the closely shaven turf. A dibber can be used for the smallest plants; an auger for larger ones. Either method is easier than trying to push through the turf with a trowel or hand-fork. Mow the grass regularly in the first year after planting (once a month is usually adequate) to prevent the new plants being smothered by tall grass. After this establishment period, during which there will be no flowers of course, the meadow will require only one or two cuts each year (depending on the vigour of the grass and the degree of tidiness required). Rake off the cut grass on at least the first cut each year.

Good tapestry planting is effective at a distance, but only reveals its full riches to detailed observation. In this tapestry of herbaceous perennials, the vivid colour of *Lychnis chalcedonica* provides the dominant note; a closer look reveals spires of veronica, teasel and verbascum.

GROUP PLANTING

Most plant catalogues advise planting in groups of three to seven plants of each kind. This advice is not only intended to sell more plants: herbaceous plants in particular look more effective when planted in substantial groups. The size of these groups will depend on the size of the garden. Three plants are adequate to make an impression in most small gardens, five or seven may be necessary in larger gardens, while groups of a dozen or more would be in order for the major borders of gardens in excess of half a hectare/one acre.

There is a tendency, for which the plant catalogues and simpler gardening books are largely to blame, to plant in even-sized blocks. This may be a satisfactory treatment for large borders of unremarkable plants in public places where time is not allocated for detailed design or skilful maintenance, but block planting creates a rather monotonous, municipal atmosphere.

Long, thin drifts are more desirable than square blocks, as drifts leave less obvious gaps in the border when they finish flowering. It is also important to avoid planting in groups of uniform size. Drifts should vary in size with the type of plant: small points of emphasis for the more spectacular plants, larger drifts of the less remarkable plants that provide the groundwork for the border. In small borders, a single plant of *Dierama pulcherrimum*, kniphofia, yucca or tall hemerocallis might provide the accent among groups of five to seven geraniums, *Anthemis tinctoria*, *Dicentra eximia* or other rounded plants. On a large scale groups of three, five or even more accent plants might be needed to create the necessary impact among a dozen or more lower, rounded plants.

In one very long border that I designed (page 46), I used as a rule of thumb 1.5m/5ft long groups as 'spots', 3m/10ft for a 'patch', 4.5-5.5m/15-18ft for a 'drift' and 6-8m/20-28ft for a 'substantial drift', and this seemed to work well.

The aim of group planting is to ensure that there is enough of each plant to create a visual impact and to combine each group with neighbours that will complement it in some way. The arching, narrow leaves and soft yellow flowers of many day-lilies, for example, look particularly good rising out of a carpet of soft purple-blue geraniums. If there is a clump or two of the tall *Campanula lactiflora* in the background to pick up the colouring of the geraniums, the effect is even better. Achilleas are useful in the garden for their finely dissected leaves and long-lasting flat plates of yellow flowers that provide a horizontal emphasis in the border. Interweaving drifts of the tall *Achillea* 'Coronation Gold' and much lower *A.* 'Moonshine' interspersed with the upright spires of pale *Kniphofia* 'Maid of Orleans' or 'Little Maid' or the white spikes of *Physostegia virginiana* 'Summer Snow' create a wonderfully cool composition. Where stronger colouring is required among the achilleas, the various forms of *Salvia nemorosa* with spikes of intense purple-blue flowers or the blue globes of hardy agapanthus are ideal.

Repetition of some of the major plants in the border is important to tie the whole scheme together, but this should not be done too regularly. Clumps of day-lilies or tall hollyhocks at 9m/30ft intervals along the border would impose a regimented effect. A more desirable balance of unity and variety is created by small tufts here and there springing from a groundwork of geraniums, with larger groups towards the back of the border interwoven with quantities of *Campanula lactiflora*, and some smaller clumps arching over the path merging almost imperceptibly into mounds of yellow achillea or *Anthemis tinctoria*.

In arranging and repeating plant groups, much can be learned from the design of Japanese gardens, particularly in relation to the powerful visual magnetism of the scalene triangle, a triangle with sides of unequal length. In the Japanese garden, a vertical rock positioned off-centre beyond a horizontal sheet of

Arranging plants in substantial groups or drifts of complementary varieties creates a satisfying visual impact. In this softly coloured autumn border, drifts of asters, sedums and polygonum flow together among the foliage of earlier-flowering plants.

SUMMER DRESS

This border, some 20m/70ft long, is planned to be in full flower during high summer and designed as a softly colour-graded scheme, from deep magenta purple at one end to white at the other.

The main backbone of the border, indeed the keynote of the colour scheme, is a small collection of rugosa roses, 'Roseraie de l'Hay', 'Hunter', 'Sarah van Fleet', the low 'Frau Dagmar Hastrup' and 'Blanc Double de Coubert', but foliage plants play an important part in emphasizing the colour scheme. The border starts with *Rosa glauca* for the sake of its blue-green foliage on strong, upright stems, then continues with widely spaced plants of the rugosas, with a break between the pink varieties and 'Blanc Double' to admit *Kolkwitzia amabilis* which produces its soft pink flowers very freely on the chalky soil of the border, the purple-stained white flowers of *Philadelphus* 'Belle Etoile' and, for flowers earlier in the season, *Syringa laciniata*.

Where the colouring is at its deepest, the border is edged with Miss Jekyll's favourite 'satin leaf', *Heuchera americana*, a trio of *Sedum telephium maximum* 'Atropurpureum' and the finer textured *Hebe* 'Bowles' Hybrid'. Around the magenta 'Roseraie de l'Hay', the theme continues with *Cotinus coggygria* 'Royal Purple' (pruned to keep it below the rose), purple berberis, the purple-leaved

forms of *Rheum palmatum* and fennel, and the vivid magenta flowers of *Geranium psilostemon,* followed by the more restrained *Penstemon* 'Garnet'. Other penstemons, some named and others acquired over the years as cuttings from friends, continue the gradation through crimson, pink and white, with sweet Williams raised from seed and selected to suit the scheme. Tall, giant-flowered cosmos were intended to do the same but, as it proved impossible to obtain self-coloured strains of seed and difficult to keep the plants long enough in pots to identify their colours, these are planted at random. The effect is better than expected as many plants are the right colour for their position while the others add a counterpoint without being dominant enough to spoil the main scheme.

Further down the border, the pink roses are matched by a very pale form of *Geranium endressii, Potentilla* 'Princess' and pink penstemons; the ground colour then changes to lavender with long drifts of catmint and the tall *Penstemon* 'Alice Hindley'. The same colour occurs in much paler tint in *Geranium renardii,* but this flowers very early and the main season of the border exploits its beautiful sage-green leaves.

This change of colouring links the pink and white roses together, but eventually the underplanting changes to white with

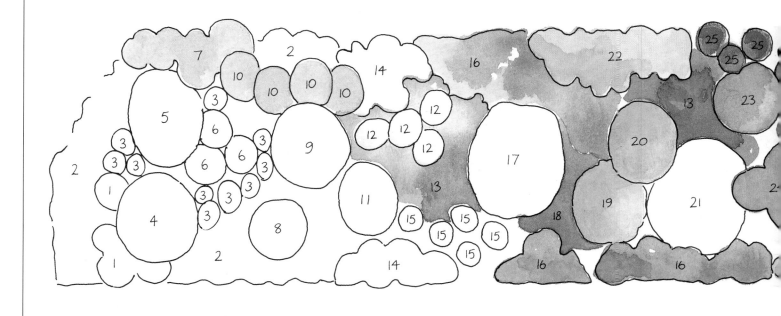

antirrhinums, *Nicotiana affinis* and *Lavatera* 'Mont Blanc' providing the connection between more varied herbaceous perennials: *Thalictrum aquilegifolium,* the ghostly *Lysimachia ephemerum,* white agapanthus and the creamy white *Clematis recta* 'Purpurea'. Scattered among this tapestry are a few white-flowered shrubs, *Potentilla* 'Vilmoriniana' with its grey leaves, the early-flowering *Osmanthus delavayi,* spring-flowering *Spiraea nipponica* 'Snowmound' (included as much for its arching, glaucous foliage as for its prolific flower) and the sweetly scented *Philadelphus microphyllus,* to give the border some structure even in the winter. The edging of the border fades from *Geranium renardii* through a greenish-white flowered form of *Sedum spectabile* to snowy white *Anaphalis nubigena,* with a few dark-leaved white antirrhinums separating the not-quite compatible sedum and anaphalis.

Many more plants could be tucked into the border and some have been: magenta *Gladiolus communis byzantinus* among the cotinus for the earlier part of the year and the very dark *Allium sphaerocephalon* for later, but the assembly of various closely related hues of a few plants – the roses, penstemons, geraniums and catmint – with the support of a few other flowering and foliage shrubs is sufficient to create a picture of real beauty for several months.

1 *Agapanthus* 'Headbourne Hybrids'
2 Antirrhinum (intermediate white)
3 *Lavatera* 'Mont Blanc'
4 *Spiraea nipponica* 'Snowmound'
5 *Osmanthus delavayi*
6 *Nicotiana affinis*
7 *Anaphalis nubigena*
8 *Potentilla* 'Vilmoriniana'
9 *Clematis recta* 'Purpurea'
10 *Lysimachia ephemerum*
11 *Philadelphus microphyllus*
12 *Thalictrum aquilegifolium*
13 Cosmos
14 *Sedum spectabile* (white)
15 Penstemons (white)
16 *Nepeta × faassenii* (catmint)
17 *Rosa rugosa* 'Blanc Double de Coubert'
18 Penstemon 'Alice Hindley'
19 *Fuchsia magellanica molinae*
20 *Potentilla* 'Princess'
21 *Philadelphus* 'Belle Etoile'
22 *Geranium renardii*
23 *Syringa laciniata*
24 Rosemary
25 Penstemons (pink)
26 *Kolkwitzia amabilis*
27 *Rosa rugosa* 'Sarah van Fleet'
28 *Rosa rugosa* 'Frau Dagmar Hastrup'
29 *Rosa rugosa* 'Hunter'
30 *Rosa rugosa* 'Rosaraie de l'Hay
31 *Geranium endressii*
32 Penstemons (red)
33 Sweet William (crimson)
34 *Geranium psilostemon*
35 *Rheum palmatum* 'Atropurpureum'
36 *Cotinus coggygria* 'Royal Purple'
37 Sweet William (magenta)
38 *Rosa glauca*
39 Fennel
40 *Penstemon* 'Garnet'
41 *Berberis thunbergii atropurpurea*
42 *Hebe* 'Bowles' Hybrid'
43 *Sedum telephium maximum* 'Atropurpureum'
44 *Heuchera americana*

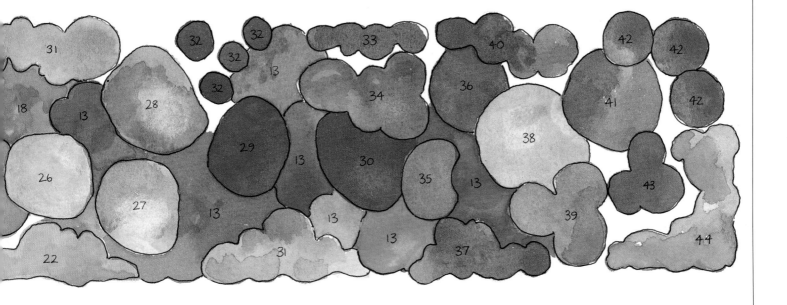

LEFT In this flower grouping, valerian and *Salvia × superba* contrast with the grey shoots of *Artemisia ludoviciana*; low pinks, *Sedum spectabile* and the slender spikes of *Linaria purpurea* 'Canon Went' add variety. Outlying plants link the group to the border as a whole.

RIGHT A broad expanse of one flower creates a memorable, if fleeting, effect. As in a natural meadow, though, what looks from a distance like a continuous sheet of poppies, on closer observation reveals myriads of enchanting details.

water creates a scalene triangle and a sense of balance is achieved that is immensely satisfying to the human eye and mind. If one scalene triangle, the rock and water for example, is balanced against another, perhaps an irregularly spaced trio of plants, the appeal of the counterpoint is even stronger.

In the flower border, arranging plants into such triangular groups and distributing the groups about the garden to form scalene triangles on a larger scale, a sense of unity similar to that experienced in the Japanese garden will be created. Grouping plants in this way leads the eye from one plant association to another and gives the impression that the whole border is full of flowers while, in fact, leaving substantial spaces for the inclusion of earlier- and later-flowering plants.

MASS PLANTING

Broad masses consisting of only one or two species create a sense of breadth; and by virtue of their simplicity they are easy to manage. There is a charm, too, in the way their ephemeral nature emphasizes the passing of the seasons – emulating the sheets of poppies, bluebells or buttercups of the fields and woods, or that moment in the year when the whole world seems to be decked with hawthorn blossom. However, they may leave unwelcome gaps in the garden when their brief season of glory is past.

Simple, mass-planted schemes have a great attraction in larger gardens where, when the flowering season is over, they can contribute welcome greenery or simply be ignored. A glade fringed with forsythias

and carpeted with early daffodils or a grove of cherries underplanted with bluebells creates a scene of breathtaking beauty when in flower, and at other times of year provides a quiet interlude in the garden.

One small and rather neglected garden I used to pass by each day was planted entirely with *Spiraea* × *vanhouttei* around a circular lawn. It was wonderful in early summer when the arching branches were wreathed in flowers, but there was also surprising charm in the delicacy of its unfolding leaves, the soft grey-green of its summer foliage, the subtle reddish-browns of autumn foliage and the warm brown of its bare winter stems, all features that might have gone unnoticed in the visual hurly-burly of a mixed planting. Most keen gardeners would have added at least some spring bulbs for early colour, perhaps a flowering tree for more height, a few herbaceous plants and an underplanting of hellebores for their winter flowers – and rightly so – but the value of simplicity in planting was powerfully demonstrated in that circle of spiraea.

Natural diversity
When viewed from a slight distance, the effect of one plant in broad masses and of many plants in a fine-textured tapestry mix is a uniformity of colouring. In nature, what looks like a mass of one flower is usually the transient result of diverse flora. Even at its peak that solid sheet of flowers dissolves on closer inspection into widely spaced groups covering only a small proportion of the total ground area.

Learning from the visual complexity of natural plant communities, it is possible to endow the mass-planted area with more than passing beauty. The easiest way to do this is to plan successive layers of mass planting in grass: *Crocus tommasinianus* in late winter could give way to small daffodils and the tall white 'Pheasant's Eye' narcissus. After the grass has been mown, the succession could continue with knapweed, field scabious and autumn crocus (whether true crocus or colchicums). The grass could then be mown for a second time.

BROAD-BRUSH PLANTING

Another way of interpreting natural diversity in the garden is with 'broad-brush planting'. In a large border, repeated groups of one plant, even though it might cover less than a tenth of the whole border, look from a short way off like a continuous, breathtaking expanse. By weaving together two or three different plants it is possible to create beautiful mosaics of colour but still to leave ample space for earlier or later combinations and to include minor incidents of attractive but less easy or less conspicuous flowers.

The season of such a scheme might start, for example, with large drifts of doronicums, early euphorbias and *Brunnera macrophylla*, progress to a sea of peonies and iris followed by day-lilies, phlox and *Campanula lactiflora* for high summer, and close in the autumn with a climax of Michaelmas daisies and the newer, garden-worthy goldenrods: a season of beauty with only ten major ingredients.

In the wonderful borders designed by Graham Stuart Thomas for Killerton Garden, Devon, early-flowering bergenias and *Hebe rakaiensis, Santolina chamaecyparissus*, the cream-flowered *S. pinnata neapolitana* and lavender were woven together for summer and *Hypericum* 'Hidcote' with striking clumps of yuccas continued the flowering season into the autumn. All these plants are evergreen or semi-evergreen so, in addition to their long flowering season, the borders provided a ground-covering sea of varying foliage textures and colours throughout the year.

A great advantage of such broad-brush planting is that maintenance is simplified. Because there are large quantities of just a few different types of plants, it is possible to time dead-heading, cutting back or

Repetition of plant forms helps to unify a planting scheme. Here repeated spires of light and dark salvias complement the arching sprays of yellow hemerocallis. The colour of the hemerocallis is subtly echoed in the foamy flowers of *Alchemilla mollis*, while occasional points of white flowers and grey foliage lighten the whole effect.

spraying for particular pests or diseases precisely to suit each one, and generally to use techniques suited to large-scale gardening. Dead-heading and end-of-season tidying might even be done with a robust hedge-trimmer, rotary mower or brush-cutter. It is also much easier to use herbicides or to find an efficient mechanical method for controlling weeds when the range of plants is limited.

If there is time to spare in the garden, it is easy to think of embellishments to the basic plan. Scattered tufts of emerging day-lily foliage provide an ideal foil for golden daffodils to harmonize with the doroni-cums, and occasional groups of hollyhocks or verbascums provide vertical accents, both valuable additions to the main scheme. In a large garden it is vital to start with a simple scheme and to develop it only if there is clearly time to maintain more complex planting, otherwise the garden will degenerate from a source of pleasure to a time-consuming chore.

In this mixed border the virtues of each plant are enhanced by those of its neighbours. Climbing roses, herbaceous valerian, annual poppies and violas mingle with alpine sedums and helianthemums in a colourful array set off by the dark green column of clipped yew.

THE MIXED BORDER

Borders that consist of one type of plant, of annuals or herbaceous perennials, are easier to manage than combinations of the two. However, each has its strengths and weaknesses, and mixtures of several plant growth types will enable you to capitalize on the advantages of each.

Flowering shrubs and trees, for example, take several years to reach any significant size but eventually grow very large unless regularly and skilfully pruned. A wide selection of shrubs is available throughout the year, but when the flowering season of each is over, it will leave a large colour gap.

Herbaceous plants, on the other hand, reach close to their ultimate height in the first year after planting and usually flower freely in that first year. Because they grow from ground level, usually starting in spring, the ultimate height of herbaceous perennials is not great in comparison with many shrubs. The main flowering season begins in early summer, although there are, of course, several attractive exceptions that flower in winter and early spring. The main disadvantages of herbaceous perennials are that they die back each autumn, leaving the ground bare and uninteresting, and that many of them need to be lifted and divided every few years if they are to be kept vigorous and free-flowering.

The merits of annuals are obvious. Their rapid growth, often to considerable heights in a short season, and their unstinting production of beautiful flowers over a comparatively long season earn them a place in most gardens. At the end of the season, though, they leave nothing but dried corpses. Painstaking ground preparation, sowing and thinning must be repeated year after year and annuals are by far the most difficult plants to protect from their near relatives, the vigorous annual weeds.

Bulbs are renowned for their brilliant flowers and many are long-lived and trouble-free garden plants, flowering bravely in late winter and early spring when there is little else of interest in the garden. However, after the welcome display of flowers comes a protracted period of dying foliage and an even longer period of bare soil, usually through the summer and autumn when the garden is most used.

In the mixed border shrubs will provide the backbone of the scheme throughout the year, with flowers in due season. Herbaceous plants fill the ground more rapidly in the garden's early years and provide a range of foliage types that cannot be matched by hardy shrubs. They also provide more detailed interest in a small garden than can be achieved with bulky shrubs, and cover the ground beneath the shrubs to reduce weed growth. A very important point is that herbaceous plants can share the ground they occupy with spring bulbs, their young foliage forming a setting for the bulbs' flowers in spring. As the bulb season finishes and the foliage starts to look unsightly, the herbaceous plants continue to grow, concealing the dying remains and producing their own attractive flowers in summer or autumn. In winter, the dying herbaceous tops are cut down and the space vacated will be furnished in turn by the emerging leaves and then the flowers of the bulbs.

The scheme could be further enriched by leaving spaces in the border for colourful annual and tender perennial plants to flower all summer long, to be pulled up at the end of the season and perhaps replaced by spring-flowering biennials and tulips. Lastly, many of the more slender and attractive climbers, annual and perennial, could be trained through shrubs and over the more robust herbaceous perennials either to harmonize with them in flower or to extend the flowering season.

The most complicated mixtures of this type would be impossible to maintain on anything other than the smallest scale, but it is in just such gardens that they are of greatest value. The shrubberies, herbaceous borders, bedding schemes and flower-draped pergolas of a large garden can be distilled into the closely stitched tapestry of the tiny flower garden – but only if one is prepared for a certain amount of physical effort and constant mental ministrations to keep the picture perfect.

LIMITED COLOUR SCHEMES

One of the most delightful features of the English flower garden at the turn of the century was the one-flower garden, a garden compartment devoted to a single flower, most commonly the rose, peony or iris. The characteristics of such gardens are exactly the same as those described for mass planting (page 64), namely a brief but spectacular display of seasonal beauty, although in the case of the rose garden, the summer-flowering season was steadily extended by the breeding of more truly perpetual flowering hybrids. The flowering season was certainly brief in iris and peony gardens, but both plants have attractive foliage (modern bearded iris are less satisfactory in this respect) and both types of garden, like the rose garden, were laid out in interesting patterns, perhaps with kerbs or low hedges to emphasize the geometry, and all three would have been liberally endowed with sculpture, sundials, seats and other supporting features. The one-flower garden was designed for seasonal glory and also to have a quieter, year-round appeal.

The one-colour garden, brought to widespread public notice by the writings of Gertrude Jekyll, bore closer resemblance to the mixed border. In Miss Jekyll's designs the one-colour border or garden was planted mainly with herbaceous perennials, liberally reinforced by half-hardy annuals such as antirrhinums, French and African marigolds, *Salvia patens* and nasturtiums. However, grey-leaved rue and tamarisk, golden holly, privet and aucuba provided the appropriate shrubby background for the colour schemes, as well as a durable framework.

The main lesson Miss Jekyll gave for the one-colour garden was not to spoil the effect for the sake of a word, not to restrict the yellow garden to yellow when small patches of blue would emphasize the

White roses, starry senecio and the tight buttons of double feverfew are emphasized by fine-textured grey-green foliage. Odd points of colour from the lavender, yellow santolina and blue delphiniums come as a pleasant surprise in what appears at first glance to be a white garden.

A VIEW FROM THE WINDOW

Designed to be enjoyed from the house in the early part of the year, this scheme, covering only a few square metres/yards, is part of a large border in a flower garden arranged around three sides of a lawn. The fourth side is partially enclosed by a small orchard underplanted with spring bulbs. The border extends away from the house towards the orchard, and the scheme here described is at the upper end of the border, seen from the house across a low-walled terrace built in orange-red brick to match adjacent walls.

Because of the predominant colour of the brickwork, the main colours of the border are orange and warm yellow, with patches of lavender-purple to complement the warmer colours and occasional white-flowered plants to lighten the effect.

Hemerocallis 'Corky'

The scheme is not well-defined in its boundaries but fades into other parts of the border with outlying groups of early flowers, and is in its turn invaded by later-flowering plants. The season begins with irregular patches of winter aconite (*Eranthis hyemalis*) among scattered groups of *Valeriana phu* 'Aurea', other groups of which link this border to more distant parts of the garden at this time. By late winter the aconites are replaced by early daffodils, the pert *Narcissus cyclamineus* hybrid, 'Tête à Tête', now flowering among the valerian foliage, the yellow-green emerging shoots of the early day-lilies (*Hemerocallis* 'Corky' and *H.* 'Golden Chimes') and white phlox, and the bright green ruffs of the faded winter aconites.

As the daffodils also fade, the scheme starts to warm up. The remarkable shrimp-pink and cream buds of *Acer pseudoplatanus* 'Brilliantissimum' and the more orange-yellow shoots of *Spiraea japonica* 'Goldflame' begin to expand and this bright leaf colour is echoed by the scented orange tulip 'General de Wet' and the golden-yellow spikes of *Cheiranthus cheiri* 'Harpur Crewe', also sweetly scented. The bright semi-evergreen leaves of this perennial wallflower, incidentally, are a cheering sight all winter long, slightly deeper in colour than *Hebe rakaiensis* next to it. To this blend of flowers and foliage are gradually added the bright orange rosettes of *Euphorbia griffithii*, emerging quite early but taking some time to grow to a height which makes them visible from a distance, and the glowing orange and yellow *Geum* 'Borisii' and *G.* 'Georgenberg', planted in a mixture at the front of the border where their close leaf-rosettes form a good edge. Finally the day lilies, with their slender flowers of rich yellow backed with tawny orange, contribute their own warm colour. These herbaceous plants are set against the backdrop of spiraea with *Berberis darwinii* and, in the distance, its more robust offspring *B.* × *stenophylla*, all adding to the orange scheme.

By early summer most of the flowers are over, but the day-lilies continue to flower for another month at least, the euphorbia retains some of its orange colouring even longer, and the phlox (*P. paniculata* 'Mia Ruys'), which provided the foliar setting for aconites and daffodils some six months earlier, produces its large white flowers to lighten the shade beneath the maple in late summer. In the first year or two after planting there was space in the border for deep orange marigolds and the much-neglected *Tithonia rotundifolia* for later colour. Although there is now no room for these annuals, the varied greens of the permanent plants provide much pleasure and a suitable setting for roses, hypericums, coreopsis, achilleas and other later flowers further down the garden, the taller ones just visible from the house over the green foreground.

1 *Berberis × stenophylla*
2 *Hypericum* 'Hidcote'
3 Roses and other summer
  flowers
4 *Euphorbia griffithii*
5 *Berberis darwinii*
6 *Spiraea japonica* 'Goldflame'
7 *Hebe rakaiensis*
8 *Bergenia cordifolia*
9 *Cheiranthus cheiri* 'Harpur
  Crewe'
10 *Phlox paniculata* 'Mia Ruys'
11 *Acer pseudoplatanus*
  'Brilliantissimum'
12 *Tulipa* 'General de Wet'
13 *Eranthis hyemalis*
14 *Narcissus cyclamineus* 'Tête à
  Tête'
15 *Hemerocallis* 'Corky' and
  H. 'Golden Chimes'
16 *Valeriana phu* 'Aurea'
17 *Geum* 'Borisii' and *G.*
  'Georgenberg'
18 *Potentilla* 'Tangerine'

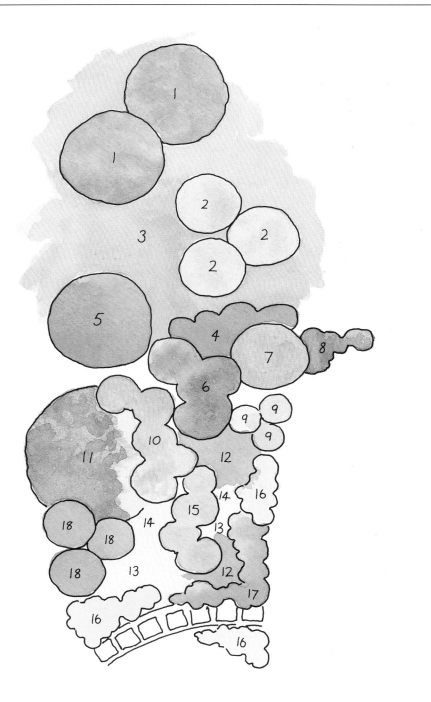

LEFT A mingling of blue and white creates a gentle and relaxing colour scheme. The solidity of clipped box sets off a delicate *Salvia interrupta*, the deeper *S.* × *superba*, delphiniums and violas with white mallows and feverfew.

RIGHT Long drifts of *Achillea* 'Moonshine' and tawny orange inula flowing around stout clumps of bicoloured kniphofias create a warm glow of harmonious colour. The narrow, spiky leaves of the kniphofia are echoed by the arching foliage of miscanthus and the mats of swordlike iris leaves bordering the path so colours and forms are skilfully woven together.

clarity of the yellow or occasional drifts of white would add sparkle to its lighter areas.

When the value of such associations is recognized, the one-colour or one-flower garden will be seen to possess considerable merits even in the smallest garden. It is possible to concentrate for a time on one particular plant and to complement it when in flower and supplement it when out of flower with other species.

On a good, alkaline loam, for example, where peonies would flourish, the peony border or garden could be underplanted with small bulbs for early spring. The peonies would reign supreme in early summer and they could lend support to lilies and clematis flowering in late summer and autumn. On lighter soils, where iris might excel, they too could be underplanted with spring bulbs and intersown with slender hardy annuals such as clarkia, gypsophila, larkspur and scabious to continue the soft colouring of the iris into high summer.

In a garden with a definite colour scheme each plant supports the others rather than vying with its neighbours for attention. With a plant or two in flower and others producing a few buds here and there, the idea of redness or whiteness or gold is readily apparent and the garden appears to be much more colourful than it really is.

Coloured foliage can play a supportive role in the border, adding strength and permanence to the scheme: grey foliage in the white garden, purple-leaved plants among fiery red and orange flowers, or golden variegated plants in the yellow border.

Colour choice

If the selection of a colour as the basis for the garden or border presents a difficulty, the concept of a one-colour planting is probably inappropriate. Some people have strong colour preferences, and their choice is reflected in their clothes, their houses and, logically, their gardens. For others the house or setting dictates a solution. Bright red brick does not flatter purples and pinks, so a garden of oranges and golden yellows would be more in keeping. Weath-

ered stone displays a multitude of subtle tints that can be picked out in associated planting, whereas white-painted walls provide the perfect backdrop for clear, bright colours: reds, blues and pink flowers with dark foliage. Around a sunny patio, grey foliage with white and soft yellow flowers picks up the lightness of the situation while, in a garden shaded by trees, the pale yellow-green leaves and white-flowers of *Campanula persicifolia alba, C. latifolia alba, Nicotiana alata,* white lilies and foxgloves not only light up the shadows but also tone with the woodland character. Around a house with large windows, colour schemes within its rooms may extend into the garden.

Greenish-white and sharp yellow flowers such as daffodils and forsythia have a cool woodland character, as does most golden foliage. Grey foliage, the chalky whites and creamy yellows have an altogether softer and warmer appearance and, when enriched with flowers of clear blue, look delightfully fresh and summery. As the quantity and depth of yellow in the scheme increases the effect becomes brighter and sunnier until it is almost offensively brassy. Deepening of the yellow tints to copper and the addition of orange and scarlet-red to the mixture creates a warmth that is intensified by the inclusion of bronze-purple foliage. Reds, purples and dark foliage create a richness of a quieter kind, the regal quality of deep velvet; many people enjoy the rich magenta purples of old roses, penstemons, foxgloves and *Geranium psilostemon*. With paler roses and geraniums, penstemons of apple-blossom pink, aquilegias, alliums and catmint, the purples and pinks fade to the softness of a lady's boudoir, merging at its palest into the grey/white theme of a white garden.

BEDDING

Bedding is a system of gardening in which formal beds are filled with massed ranks of plants for temporary display: half-hardy annuals and tender perennials for summer followed by biennials and bulbs to flower in spring. As a system it reached its peak in the late nineteenth century, in great architectural gardens planted with tens of thousands of brilliantly coloured tender perennials arranged in elaborate geometric patterns. Gardeners of today could profitably take inspiration from the inventive geometry and good colour planning to be found in old gardening books to experiment with bedding schemes.

The most successful schemes rely on simple patterns and harmonious colour groupings: clear yellow with a little complementary blue; white and blue flowers with grey foliage; crimson and copper; or a glowing blend of yellow, orange and scarlet. One of my favourite schemes in recent years has been

RIGHT An intriguing geometry of spiralling box hedges ensure that this parterre is interesting even when there is not a flower to be seen. A filling of nasturtiums transforms the beds into a richly coloured brocade. Although such schemes are usually associated with the great formal gardens of the seventeenth and nineteenth centuries, they are readily adapted to the modern front garden.

LEFT Smaller-flowered varieties of French marigold make ideal edging for the flower border. Their finely cut foliage and neatly proportioned flowers create a precise yet charmingly informal effect.

a groundwork of white petunias with bands of green love-lies-bleeding (*Amaranthus caudatus*) through the spines of the beds and a single huge-leaved castor oil plant (*Ricinus communis*) in the centre of each bed.

Past examples have much to teach about the importance of the shape of beds, which should provide interest even when empty, and the value of low hedges, clipped greens and other permanent features to support the garden in lean periods.

Bedding plants

Formal displays of bedding plants will only succeed in open, sunny situations and on reasonably fertile soils. With partial shade from a building or, worse, the shade and roots of nearby trees, the plants will grow and flower unevenly and the effect will be ruined. However, 'bedding plants' may, of course, be used in other ways. Plants such as pelargoniums, petunias, lobelias, salvias and French marigolds, which have come to be regarded automatically as bedding plants, are of great value also in a mixed border, particularly in a small garden: with their long season of bright, clear colour, they will reinforce the colour schemes of the border throughout the summer months. Gertrude Jekyll, in her own garden and in the many plans she made for others, used quantities of

bedding plants – soft-coloured ageratum, heliotrope and China asters, but also vivid marigolds and scarlet salvias – woven among herbaceous perennials and shrubs in informal flower borders.

Spaces left in the mixed border for summer annuals or tender perennials can be filled in the autumn with groups of biennials and bulbs to flower in the spring. Each group should be chosen to associate with adjacent perennial plants: red wallflowers, polyanthus or double daisies among the crimson young shoots of peonies or purple-leaved phlox, tawny orange wall-flowers in front of the red-gold foliage of *Spiraea japonica* 'Goldflame', or blue forget-me-nots with the sharp yellow leaves of day-lilies, *Valeriana phu* 'Aurea' or *Euphorbia polychroma*. When these spring flowers have finished they can be pulled up and replaced with summer bedding plants to harmonize with later-flowering perennials and summer foliage.

The wide range of foliage plants used for 'sub-tropical' bedding in the nineteenth century should not be forgotten when creating a setting for the flowers. Blue-leaved eucalyptus, feathery *Grevillea robusta* and *Jacaranda ovalifolia,* and *Canna indica* and *Rhus communis* with their huge leaves are but a few of the dozens of good plants available.

On all but the smallest scale, formal bedding requires large numbers of plants: even a small garden will easily absorb a hundred. At garden centre prices, the outlay could be considerable. However, for those with the interest but without the money, it is not difficult to raise plants at home. With a small heated frame, some capillary matting and using pelleted seeds in compartmented seed trays to avoid pricking out, the necessary quantities can be raised in a small space with relatively little effort.

Bedding plants are often confined to tight geometrical patterns, but here long-flowering heliotrope, cosmos and spidery cleome blend easily into the freer form of a herbaceous border with catmint, Japanese anemone, erigeron, *Campanula lactiflora* 'Loddon Anna', *Astilbe chinensis davidii,* and the distinctive crooked spikes of *Lysimachia clethroides.* The small patch of magenta-pink impatiens in the foreground enlivens the scheme.

CONTAINER GARDENING

Pots, tubs, window boxes and urns provide additional growing space for plants and can themselves be attractive features in the garden. They also make it possible to move plants around, to grow plants that would not otherwise flourish in the garden, and to grow plants which are not fully hardy in the area. For those whose only outside space is a rooftop or balcony, containers offer the opportunity to enjoy the flower garden to the limits that practicality and imagination allow. In a small paved garden, where access to the native soil is restricted, it makes sense to use every scrap of soil available for permanent planting that will soften the hard appearance of the paving, and to grow the more ephemeral plants in containers.

An advantage of plants in containers is that they are relatively mobile. Even heavy pots can be moved with care, using sack-trucks or castors. In a small garden, therefore, it is possible to grow a range of plants that may be interesting for a short season and to place them in strategic positions when they are at their best. I try to have a succession of plants available so that there are always two or three on the front doorstep. In the winter, large- and small-leaved ivies complement the winter flowers growing nearby in narrow borders; small pots of early bulbs soon follow, then tulips (especially the beautifully scented 'General De Wet', whose orange flowers look lovely against the brickwork). As summer advances, tender plants are moved out of the greenhouse: osteospermums, the coloured-leaved pelargoniums and fuchsias, for example, but there is also a changeable supply of plants that would grow satisfactorily in the garden itself – lilies, *Euphorbia characias wulfenii*, and the white arum lily, *Zantedeschia aethiopica*. One of my favourites, an idea borrowed from Gertrude Jekyll, is maiden's wreath, *Francoa ramosa*. From rosettes of gently toothed leaves it produces long wands of pink-veined white flowers starting in early summer (later in the open garden) and continuing to flower for a month or more. As the seed pods arch and sway gently over the leaves, it is often still on the doorstep in early autumn.

Wanting to use attractive pots can be reason enough for growing plants in them. Sometimes the pots are needed as part of the scheme, to provide architectural solidity and regularity, in which case the pots themselves should not be obscured by flowering plants and the plants should be of permanent interest, in keeping with the character of the garden as a whole. In large pots and boxes it is possible to grow climbers and quite large shrubs or even small trees. Often, though, one simply acquires pots because they are attractive and the plants for them can be chosen with a free hand. Even weather-proof pots can be severely damaged in winter if wet soil in them freezes, so it is useful insurance to bring the better pots inside during the winter.

Growing plants in pots allows the soil to be modified at will: rhododendrons and camellias can be grown in a chalk garden and the lime-loving clematis in gardens with acid sand or clay. This artificial situation is generally more successful than preparing a site in the garden: the plant in the pot obviously needs watering and feeding, so gets it and flourishes, whereas the rhododendron in a peat-filled hole in the chalk only receives attention when it shows signs of distress, which is usually too late.

Drainage, or lack of it, is another important aspect of the garden and drainage problems can be circumvented by growing plants in pots. Pelargoniums and other tender perennials flower more freely in the drier conditions afforded by pots than in the garden and many marginally hardy plants survive in pots because of the free drainage. On the other hand, moisture-demanding plants can flourish in a dry garden if they are grown in pots standing in saucers of water.

Growing tender or half-hardy plants is one of the greatest joys of container gardening. Oleander, eucalyptus and *Albizia julibrissin* are three plants which I grow in large pots. The albizia might just grow outside, but it comes into its finely-cut leafage much earlier if overwintered in the greenhouse, and I am hoping it will produce its pink powder puff flowers at an earlier age if the roots are confined. Summer bulbs are also a great delight. Again, tigridias and other exotic-looking flowers are produced earlier and more freely if started in pots; and the process of drying them off for a winter rest is under complete control, as the pots can simply be laid on their sides, the dead leaves pulled off the plants when they are dry, and the bulbs stored in the dry soil where they are less prone to shrivelling and decay than if lifted from the garden and stored in bags.

Zonal pelargoniums, the shrubby calceolarias, fuchsias, *Argyranthemum frutescens* and many other tender perennials are superb in pots, alone or in combination, and will often flower well into the winter if the pots are moved into a sunny room, or ideally a conservatory, in the autumn before there is any danger of frost. The same applies, of course, to fibrous-rooted begonias, impatiens and many other so-called half-hardy annual bedding plants that are, in fact, tender perennials.

One plant which has become popular in recent years is *Bidens atrosanguinea* (or *Cosmos atrosanguineus*). The prolific crimson flowers and dusky foliage have their own quiet charm – and the flowers smell exactly like chocolate! This plant can be grown in the garden during the summer, but it is generally much more successful in a pot, with liberal watering and feeding. In the autumn it can be moved into a frost-free place and dried off completely until it decides for itself to start into growth in the spring. For scent, seductive charm and ease of management, it is an ideal container plant.

Ivy-leaved pelargoniums are ideal plants for containers, producing an endless display of flowers in response to the restricted root-room and higher soil temperature. Here the soft colours of the pelargoniums are echoed by trailing verbena and grey spikes of curry plant (*Helichrysum angustifolium*). All can be moved into a sunny room or conservatory before frost threatens, to continue their display into the winter.

FLOWERING PLANTS

The plants described in this chapter have been chosen for their balance between different soil types and situations, to provide flowers throughout the year and in a balanced range of colours and heights. The lists include enough plants to furnish a variety of flower gardens without bemusing the beginner and they may introduce experienced gardeners to some good but neglected plants with which they may not be familiar.

Considerable attention has already been given to the importance of foliage as a setting for the flower garden and foliage quality has been important in deciding what to include here. Some popular plants, such as the lupin, have been excluded because, although its foliage is lovely in the early part of the year, the whole plant becomes bedraggled soon after flowering.

Plants have been grouped by growth form, as hardy annuals, herbaceous perennials and so on, but this is not as simple as it sounds. Categories were made by man, not nature, and many good plants fall between artificial divisions.

The distinction between hardy and half-hardy annuals depends on local climate, some of the plants traditionally raised as half-hardy annuals being suitable for sowing outside after all danger of frost has passed in warmer, sheltered zones. Many plants traditionally grown as tender perennials and over-wintered as rooted cuttings each year can now be raised as half-hardy annuals from seed.

Other plants have fleshy rootstocks. They are not bulbs in the botanical sense of the word but they can be lifted when they have finished growing, then stored dry and sold as 'bulbs' through bulb catalogues and in garden shops. Agapanthus and eremurus are good examples. Although available as dried 'bulbs', they will be established in the flower garden more reliably if bought as herbaceous plants in moist soil. Several true bulbs or corms suffer if they are dried for too long, cyclamen in particular, and it is common to see these, together with camassia, crocosmia and galtonia, offered for sale as herbaceous plants.

Some plants are particularly useful because they combine the characteristics of two or three plant groups. Many sub-shrubs, for example, are exceptionally free-flowering and long-flowering plants because they come from parts of the world where they are seldom exposed to frost or drought. In cool climates, they are midway between shrubs and herbaceous perennials. The hardiest may grow into large shrubs in sheltered gardens while others can be planted deeply for winter protection and cut to the ground each autumn like herbaceous perennials. More tender varieties still may need to be overwintered as rooted cuttings under glass while plant breeders are now producing varieties that flower quickly from seed and can be raised as half-hardy annuals.

Plants that are difficult to categorize have been grouped with their nearest kin with an indication of when they may be used in other ways.

To avoid repetition of cultural requirements, it may be safely assumed that the plants described will grow well in a wide range of garden soils and in sun or semi-shade. Only if a plant has particular requirements are these indicated.

Colour, form, texture and seasonal considerations are all important when choosing plants. Here, spikes of delphiniums and round heads of *Campanula lactiflora* have finished their main display, but secondary buds promise later colour. Heliopsis and deep orange alstroemerias now create glowing colour, while feathery goldenrod, *Macleaya microcarpa* and slender trails of clematis will continue the flowering season into the autumn.

HARDY ANNUALS

In general, hardy annuals are sown in spring where they will flower and the seedlings are thinned out to produce sturdy, well branched plants. When this cannot be done (perhaps the soil is in a window box which is full of spring bulbs) they can be raised in small pots or, better still, in cellular propagating trays to avoid root disturbance when transplanting. Some annuals are sufficiently hardy that they can be sown in autumn to overwinter as small plants and produce more flowers on larger plants earlier in the following year than they would have done from spring sowing.

Note: * indicates those annuals hardy enough to sow outside in the autumn.

AGROSTEMMA githago*

Corncockle
H:75cm/30in   S:20cm/8in
This tall, graceful annual, a weed of the cornfields, has large, single, pale-lilac flowers on slender but strong stems. If dead flowers are removed it has a long flowering season; otherwise it will finish flowering by late summer.

It is an excellent plant for the annual border, either in drifts, in a mixture with other flowering annuals or in a wild flower meadow mixture to provide colour in the first year. Sown among perennials and shrubs, it associates especially well with grey foliage and pale flowers. If sown late, in ground vacated by spring biennials or among bearded iris after their flowering, it provides later colour on shorter plants.

CALENDULA officinalis*

Pot marigold
H:30–60cm/12–24in   S:30–45cm/12–18in
One of the easiest plants to grow from outdoor sowing in spring or autumn, its seed is also large enough to be sown individually in small pots. Dead flowers should be removed to ensure a long flowering season.

Calendula refers to the fact it may flower at any time of the year, *officinalis* signifies medicinal uses and the 'pot' of its common name refers to its medieval use in soups and stews. Given these attributes and the fact that it will flourish in poor, dry soil, it is not surprising that this marigold, also known as St Mary's gold, is one of the best-loved of flowers. Modern varieties are fully double, dwarf or tall, in a wide range of colours: sulphur-yellow and apricot for pastel groupings among grey foliage or bronze-tinged varieties such as 'Fiesta Gitana' and especially the glowing orange-brown 'Indian Prince' for associating with bronze foliage and other brilliant flowers.

CENTAUREA cyanus*

Cornflower
H:30–75cm/12–30in   S:15cm/6in
The cornflower has long been grown in gardens for its clear blue flowers on stiffly upright plants with fine textured foliage. It will grow in the poorest soil but, given reasonable garden soil, will produce vigorous plants flowering into the autumn from spring sowing.

It is ideal for the annual border, for sowing in mixtures, for temporary colour in wild flower meadow mixtures and for inclusion in the mixed border. The delicacy of the flowers is accentuated when grown in thin drifts among silvery foliage or deep red flowers. Low-growing varieties are available in a wide colour range including white, pink, red and purple. Sown in large masses and edged with silver foliage these make charming

Calendula officinalis

Convolvulus tricolor

features in the flower garden.

C. moschata, the sweet sultan, is a little known annual, similar to cornflower but with a sweet scent and wide colour range, including yellow.

CHRYSANTHEMUM species

There are three equally useful species of annual chrysanthemum, all of which flower all summer and autumn.

C. carinatum, tricoloured chrysanthemum (H:60cm/24in; S:30cm/12in), is a much-branched plant with tricoloured flowers banded with white, crimson and yellow. It is a cheerful addition to the annual or mixed border.

C. coronarium, crown daisy (H:90cm/36in; S:45cm/18in), is taller and much more vigorous with finely cut foliage and flowers that are usually a clear, bright yellow, although a white variety is available. It is large enough to provide substance in new gardens, filling in between newly planted shrubs and associating especially well with variegated cornus.

C. segetum, corn marigold (H:45cm/18in; S:15cm/6in), is more slender, clear yellow and especially useful in the annual border or wild flower meadow.

CLARKIA elegans*

Clarkia
H:75cm/30in   S:15cm/6in
Sown in autumn or spring in reasonable soil these make tall, slender plants with delicately frilled flowers in a wide range of soft colours, pink, white, rose and purple, throughout the summer.

Clarkia is typical of the summer annuals in its soft colouring, freedom of flowering and ease of cultivation. It is wonderful in borders of mixed annuals, among grey foliage and pastel coloured perennials in the mixed border. It is also slender enough to be sown among clumps of iris to provide flowers when the iris have finished their short season.

Delphinium ajacis

CONVOLVULUS tricolor

Annual convolvulus
H:30cm/12in   S:30cm/12in
Sown in situ in spring, this wide spreading, bushy plant produces a long succession of funnel-shaped flowers with brilliant blue rims, white within a clear, soft-yellow eye, and bright green foliage.

It is versatile, as an edging plant for the blue border, with soft or bright yellow and orange flowers such as the Californian poppies and layia among annuals, or with *Anthemis tinctoria, Achillea* 'Moonshine' and montbretia in the perennial border. It will add a point of brilliance among grey foliage, but it should be kept away from soft pinks and mauves.

DELPHINIUM ajacis

Rocket larkspur
H:45–120cm/18–48in   S:20–35cm/8–15in
The annual delphinium produces tall, tapering spires of graceful flowers in shades of purple, pink and white over finely cut dark foliage. Given good cultivation, the tall varieties make majestic additions to the mixed border, but the newer, dwarf varieties are also useful for their vertical accent without the need for staking.

Uses are similar to those of *Clarkia elegans,* with which it associates especially well.

ESCHSCHOLZIA californica

Californian poppy
H:35cm/15in   S:35cm/15in
In well-drained soil and in full sun the Californian poppy grows quickly into a mound of finely dissected, grey-green foliage spangled with a succession of translucent flowers. Modern varieties have flowers of glowing orange and crimson, the individual flowers single or semi-double and irregularly marked with lighter and darker stripes. The effect is brilliant but never garish, although the clear orange of older varieties is hard to beat.

They are ideal at the edge of the border and look effective among upright kniphofias, crocosmias and hemerocallis.

The much smaller *E. caespitosa,* sold as 'Miniature Primrose', has sulphur-yellow flowers over grey foliage and is lovely with catmint, lavender and other grey-blue plants.

IBERIS umbellata

Candytuft
H:25cm/10in   S:20cm/8in
With domed heads of scented flowers in shades of pink, deep carmine, lavender and white over low-growing, compact, dark green foliage, candytuft is a useful and easily grown plant for the foreground of annual borders or for edging mixed borders. *Iberis amara* is a taller species with longer flowerheads of brilliant chalky whiteness. Both species associate well with clarkia and larkspur.

LIMNANTHES douglasii∗

H:15cm/6in   S:15cm/6in
An adaptable plant, growing best in a dry, sunny situation, limnanthes forms a dense carpet of neatly toothed dark green leaves and five-petalled flowers, deep lemon centred with a broad white margin. It is fragrant and attractive to bees. Its low, spreading habit makes it an ideal edging plant for the mixed border, spilling over the edge of pots or in patches in the rock garden. On fertile soils it will seed itself and smother more delicate plants.

LOBULARIA maritima

Sweet alyssum
H:5–15cm/2–6in   S:5–20cm/2–8in
This easily grown annual is commonly associated with blue lobelia as an edging, usually to scarlet salvias or zonal geraniums, but the effect is almost inevitably uneven as alyssum flourishes in hot, dry summers and lobelia in cool, wet ones.

Sown in situ and thinned into small clumps of seedlings, the upright 'Little Dorrit' makes a neat, white edging, firmer than Virginian stock or linaria. 'Carpet of Snow' makes wide compact hummocks; 'Oriental Night' is of similar habit but has flowers of deep crimson-purple, a striking contrast to its white counterpart but harmonizing beautifully with *Penstemon* 'Garnet', purple sage and other plants of similar flower or foliage colour.

MALCOLMIA maritima∗

Virginian stock
H:15cm/6in   S:5cm/2in
The most slender of the annuals, this has delicately veined, four-petalled flowers in pink, white, lavender and red on frail, branching stems. If sown thinly where it is to flower, it needs no further thinning to produce a tapestry of unifying softness.

MENTZELIA lindleyi

H:45cm/18in   S:45cm/18in
Although only suitable for an open, sunny situation, mentzelia (also known as *Bartonia aurea*) is a useful annual, flowering over an unusually long period. The pointed ends to its five petals and the rounded mass of yellow stamens in the centre add delicacy to the otherwise bold, brilliant yellow flowers; the glaucous character of the finely toothed leaves ensures that it associates as well with lavender, rosemary and other soft colours as it does with the golds and oranges that it usually partners.

LEFT *Eschscholzia californica*
RIGHT *Limnanthes douglasii*

Nigella damascena

NIGELLA damascena*

Love-in-a-mist
H:45cm/18in   S:15cm/6in

The common name aptly describes the effect of pale, fringed, grey-blue flowers nestling in finely dissected pale green foliage. Its less-used name, devil-in-the-bushes, refers to the intriguing spiny, inflated seed heads that follow the flowers. Easily grown and hardy, nigella associates perfectly with grey foliage, pale yellow or white flowers, mixing well with other annuals or standing on its own in generous groups in the mixed border.

'Miss Jekyll', with clear blue flowers on tall plants, is the most popular variety, but other modern varieties have pink, white, dark and light blue flowers on smaller plants, also useful where more varied colouring is required. Both look good with the more solid mounds of purple, pink or white petunias or violas in the foreground.

PAPAVER rhoeas*

Poppy
H:75cm/30in   S:20cm/8in

The brilliant scarlet colouring, crumpled silk petals and extreme delicacy of its slender stems endow the poppy of the cornfields with particular charm. Easily grown, it is especially useful for temporary effect in wild flower meadows.

Shirley poppies, with delicate pink, white and crimson two-toned flowers are even more useful among other annuals or as repeated drifts through the mixed border.

P. commutatum 'Lady Bird' has flowers of deep scarlet-crimson with a black blotch at the base of each petal, a perfect companion for *Lobelia cardinalis* and the dark and much heavier dahlias. The bold grey leaves and faded purple-pink flowers of the double *P. somniferum* associate beautifully with old roses, geraniums and other dusky flowers.

Papaver rhoeas 'Shirley Hybrids'

RESEDA odorata

Mignonette
H:30cm/12in   S:15cm/6in
If the seeds are pressed into a firm, moist seedbed without burying them mignonette will grow easily. Near the front of a border its fluffy green flower spikes, red-tinged in some varieties, add a quiet distinction and a powerful honeylike fragrance to the flower garden.

It should be near, but not spilling over, the edge of the border as the plant itself has an unpleasant smell when brushed or picked. A foreground of alyssum (also sweetly scented), limnanthes, or London pride will achieve the desired separation.

SALVIA horminum (syn. Salvia viridis)

Clary
H:45cm/18in   S:15cm/6in
Clary is as far removed from its well-known relative the scarlet bedding salvia as it is possible to be: a slender, upright plant with small grey-green leaves and whitish flowers enclosed in large bracts of soft pink, purple-blue or white. It is these soft-coloured bracts that give the plant its colour, which lasts over a very long season.

The soft colouring and pungent aroma associate well with other herbs, notably purple sage, with old roses and other plants of muted colouring.

SCABIOSA atropurpurea*

Sweet scabious
H:100cm/40in   S:45cm/18in
The best plants, flowering freely from early summer until autumn, are produced by sowing the large seeds singly in small pots in autumn, overwintering in a cold frame and planting out in spring. Smaller plants with later flowers can be obtained by sowing outside in spring.

The elegant pincushion flowers in white, pink, lavender, crimson and deep maroon are sweetly scented and attractive to butterflies. They mix well with other annuals of soft colouring but are particularly lovely with shrub roses of muted purple-red or buff-yellow.

HALF-HARDY ANNUALS

Half-hardy annuals are those that will not survive frost; they need longer to reach flowering size than they would get if sown in the open ground, so they are started off under glass, sometimes in midwinter, and planted out when all danger of frost has passed. They therefore entail more effort than the hardy annuals but flower over a much longer season. In the mildest areas, the fastest growing of the half-hardy annuals can be sown outside much later than the truly hardy annuals and will flower in late summer and autumn.

Note: * indicates plants hardy enough to be sown outdoors in early summer to flower in late summer and autumn.

Antirrhinum majus

AGERATUM houstonianum

H:15–45cm/6–18in S:15–30cm/6–12in
Best suited to a sunny situation, ageratums will tolerate some shade. They have compact, pyramidal heads of fluffy blue-grey flowers and wide grey-green leaves. The compact bedding varieties, often of a deeper blue, provide a firm edge to the bed or border, associating in formal patterns or informal drifts with white or pale yellow petunias or antirrhinums, yellow-flowered rue or pale pink penstemons. The swordlike leaves of *Iris pallida* 'Aurea Variegata' emerging from the cloudy tufts of ageratum also create a delightful accent at the corner of a border. The looser-growing varieties blend gracefully with soft coloured plants in the middle border.

AMARANTHUS caudatus*

Love-lies-bleeding
H:75cm/30in S:50cm/20in
This needs a moist soil, as its large leaves soon wilt in dry conditions. Its long, drooping racemes of dusky-red flowers and large, bronze-tinged leaves create a sumptuous effect but, because of its strik-

ing form, it needs careful placement to avoid looking coarse. Its velvety richness is shown to the full among old roses, perhaps with purple-leaved fennel as a lighter foil, with an edging of bold-leaved bergenias or intermingled with crimson dahlias and purple-leaved cotinus.

The pale green form is equally striking, either with sharp yellow flowers such as calceolaria or *Coreopsis verticillata,* or in cool green and white schemes. With an edging of white petunias and accents of pale green *Ricinus communis* it makes a good long-lasting partnership.

ANTIRRHINUM majus

Snapdragon
H:15–120cm/6–48in S:20–45cm/8–18in
The wide colour range – white, yellow, orange, pink, red, almost black-crimson, lilac and bicolours – and its range of height from towering spires to dumpy dwarfs make the antirrhinum a candidate for both formal bedding and informal colour-graded borders. Penstemon-flowered

types are even more colourful but they have lost the elegance of the more open antirrhinum spike and its amusing capacity for animation.

Because of its vast range it is difficult to single out good companions. However, lemon and white over blue lobelia, ivory white with catmint, orange with the pale blue forms of *Anchusa azurea, Salvia patens* or lobelia, and deep crimson with the purple leaves of *Heuchera americana,* dwarf *Berberis thunbergii* or *Sedum maximum* give some idea of its versatility.

CALLISTEPHUS chinensis

China aster
H:15–75cm/6–30in S:20–45cm/8–18in
This is one of the most important late summer and autumn annuals. Tight hummocks covered in double flowers have been produced for bedding and for use as travel-tolerant pot plants, but the chief joy among China asters lies in the taller and laxer plants, whether with tight, pincushion flowers, elegant incurving singles or huge, spidery-petalled ostrich plume

types. The colour range is wide but soft: white, pink, lavender, purple and red with an occasional creamy yellow, all of which associate beautifully with the smaller flowers of the true asters (Michaelmas daisies), the flat pink domes of *Sedum spectabile,* the second flowering of catmint and with silvery-leaved artemisias.

CLEOME spinosa

Spider plant
H:1.2m/4ft   S:75cm/30in
With its strong, upright growth and large five- to seven-fingered leaves, cleome is one of the few annuals that looks as permanent as a shrub. It needs reasonable soil and adequate moisture to give of its best but is useful for creating an instant impression of substance in a new garden. The flowers, ranging from white to deep pink emerging continually from the summit of a dome-shaped cluster, are as graceful as the plant is robust.

COSMOS bipinnatus

Cosmea
H:1.2m/4ft   S:90cm/36in
With large mounds of feathery, dark green foliage topped by huge single daisies of deep crimson, deep or light pink or white on stiff stems, annual cosmos is the epitome of cottage-garden charm. The main stem needs careful staking and side branches are liable to snap off in windy situations but, among roses and other shrubs, the whole plant is rigid enough to stand up without further support.

Cosmos associates well with tall delphiniums, the lesser spires of penstemons or the more solid lavateras.

DELPHINIUM grandiflorum

Chinese delphinium
H:40cm/15in   S:20cm/8in
This slender delphinium, often called *D. chinense,* has deeply divided, dark green leaves and spikes of widely spaced flowers

Cosmos bipinnatus

of a brilliant blue. In mild areas it may overwinter as a short-lived perennial but it is much better when raised from seed each year. It must be guarded from slugs.

The flowers show up well among grey foliage, but clash with lavender or similarly coloured flowers. This plant appears brilliant, though not conspicuous from a distance, among crimson flowers and dark purple foliage.

DIANTHUS caryophyllus, D. chinensis

Annual carnations and pinks
H:20–45cm/8–18in   S:20cm/8in
The annual carnations are elegant plants, producing a continuous array of flowers in a wide range of delicate colours on slender stems over mats of silvery foliage in late summer and autumn. They are ideal edging plants for the grey border, best appreciated in long drifts but also attractive individually, arching out from small spaces among lavender, rue or iris.

Annual pinks have single flowers nest-

ling close to the dome of foliage. The flowers of newer varieties tend to have a harshness and vividness of colouring that makes them difficult to use but the softer coloured varieties are ideal for creating a firm edge to large drifts of Virginian stock, love-in-a-mist or cornflowers.

LAVATERA trimestris∗

Mallow
H: 75cm/30in   S:45cm/18in
Although easily grown as a hardy annual, mallow responds well to sowing singly in small pots under glass and planting out as well-established young plants. Then it will start to flower in early summer and continue unabated until frost, producing hundreds of large, funnel-shaped flowers in clear pink or, in the case of 'Mont Blanc', the most brilliant white, faintly tinged with pink in the eye of the flower.

This flower is perfect for the white garden, for lightening the middle of mixed borders and for large pots, especially with woolly-leaved *Helichrysum petiolare* climb-

ing up into it and trailing down over the sides of the pot. Pink-flowered varieties also look good with grey foliage and lavender, purple or white flowers.

LOBELIA erinus

Lobelia
H:15cm/6in   S:10cm/4in
Given adequate moisture, lobelia will flower with unabated freedom from early summer until destroyed by frost. The colour range includes white, reddish purple and deep purple, often with contrasting white eyes, in addition to the pale and deep clear blues with which it is usually associated. A planting of mixed colours as an edging to petunias, penstemons or other flowers with a similar colour range is attractive. The clear pale and deep blues with yellow or white antirrhinums or petunias are delightfully refreshing. Pale blue trailing lobelia is lovely, too, with pale orange begonias, and contrasts well with the dark crimson flowers of *Cosmos atrosanguineus*.

NICOTIANA alata

Tobacco
H:30–90cm/12–36in   S:30–60cm/ 12–24in
The original species is a large, softly hairy plant with white flowers opening in early evening and throughout the night to release its marvellous fragrance. In good soil with adequate moisture it will grow even in shaded situations, where the flowers stay open for much of the day too. Breeding has extended the colour range to pink, red, mauve, cream and green and modern varieties have flowers that stay open during the day but these lack the heady perfume of the old white form.

The dwarf varieties flower freely at a uniform height, and are attractive among coppery foliage and red-purple flowers but the looser growth of the taller varieties is preferable where space is available.

Lobelia erinus

PETUNIA hybrids

H:20–35cm/8–15in   S:35cm/15in

Among the most intensively hybridized of all annuals, the petunia is available in an immense range of self-colours in addition to striped, frilled and double forms. Many of the single varieties are so bright that they lend themselves only to the most vivid bedding schemes, but there are hosts of more subtle colours, white and pale yellow, soft pinks, rich reds and scented dusky purples that flower all summer and autumn above their soft grey-green foliage. Older varieties, with their semi-trailing habit, are particularly useful for spilling out of pots and window boxes or scrambling into roses, berberis, rosemary and other twiggy shrubs to create a wide variety of colour harmonies. The doubles are too heavy to thrive out of doors in wet climates.

SALVIA splendens

Scarlet salvia

H:20–35cm/8–15in   S:15–30cm/6–12in

To produce good plants, the salvia must be pricked off soon after germination and grown individually in small pots for planting out in summer. Each year brings more compact varieties with brighter scarlet flowers on deeper green foliage. Green is the safest accompaniment, soft mounds of *Kochia scoparia* or plumes of green amaranthus, perhaps with an edging of curled parsley. Combining drifts of salvia with scarlet lychnis, red and yellow kniphofias and crimson-scarlet dahlias in a setting of bronze cannas and other purple foliage will absorb the fierce scarlet into a fiery richness.

The newer deep purple and faded pink varieties should not be mixed with the scarlet but they are attractive and long-lasting components of magenta-purple colour schemes, together with grey or purple foliage.

Tagetes signata

TAGETES erecta, T. patula*

African and French marigold

H:20–75cm/8–30in   S:15–45cm/6–18in

These plants are widely used for bedding, with single or fully double flowers, quilled, crimped or fluted in pale lemon, deep yellow, orange or glowing tawny red and yellow combinations, the flowers almost covering the dark green dissected foliage from early summer to late autumn. The smaller and simpler single or crested forms are valuable additions to the flower border among taller heleniums, orange kniphofias and pale blue flowers. The still more slender *Tagetes signata*, in its pale yellow form, looks lovely among deep blue flowers – lobelia, *Salvia patens* and *Delphinium grandiflorum,* for example.

TITHONIA rotundifolia

Mexican sunflower

H:100cm/40in   S:75cm/30in

This neglected annual is easily grown, producing large, leafy plants with quantities of bright orange-scarlet flowers, similar to single dahlias in appearance, in late summer and autumn. It is useful for the back of the border where it will pick up the colour of crocosmias, kniphofias, phygelius and late-flowering hemerocallis. Although bright, the colour is soft enough to combine dramatically with dark purple *Clematis × durandii, C. × jackmanii* or *C. viticella.*

ZINNIA elegans *

H:15–75cm/6–30in   S:20–60cm/8–24in

Contrary to its specific name, the modern zinnia is anything but elegant. Breeders have concentrated on tightly double flowers in bright colours on vigorous, sturdy plants. Varieties offered to the amateur are almost exclusively of garish mixed colours. However, the flowers of intermediate varieties are splendid, freely produced in a hot summer and long-lasting. Zinnias grow quickly from seed so they can be sown individually in pots and selected for particular schemes when the colour can be identified.

Tender Perennials

Tender perennials are killed by frost but may be overwintered as rooted cuttings in a frost-free greenhouse and planted out in early summer to give a continuous display of flowers until frosts return.

The distinction between these and the half-hardy annuals is hazy and the range of tender perennials that can be grown as half-hardy annuals has increased. However, there are still many good old varieties that must be propagated by cuttings and, if a particularly good plant occurs in a batch of seed-raised plants, this can be propagated by cuttings to preserve it.

ARGYRANTHEMUM frutescens (syn. CHRYSANTHEMUM frutescens)

H:75cm/30in   S:60cm/24in
This semi-shrubby chrysanthemum is overwintered as young plants rooted from cuttings in late summer. The deeply lobed grey leaves are topped by a succession of wide-rayed daisies with a pincushion centre. The arching stems of 'Jamaica Primrose' (pale yellow) or 'Mary Wootton' (white with a pink eye) are lovely among grey foliage and other pastel flowers.

A.f. foeniculaceum is a tender shrub, easily propagated by cuttings and growing a metre/yard high and wide in a summer, producing hundreds of small, white daisies over silver-grey leaves and stems. Best grown in pots, it combines well with pale pink zonal pelargoniums, trailing lobelia, *Convolvulus althaeoides* or *Plecostachys serpyllifolia*.

BEGONIA hybrids

H:15–30cm/6–12in   S:15–30cm/6–12in
Begonia semperflorens, the fibrous begonia, is a favourite bedding and pot plant with numerous small white, pink or red flowers over glossy green or bronze foliage. It is usually grown as a half-hardy annual but cuttings root easily or plants may be lifted to overwinter in pots. Its compact habit and freedom of flowering make it an excellent choice for geometrical bedding, pots and window boxes but it can also be used informally at the edge of mixed borders. The dark-leaved, scarlet-flowered hybrids underline the theme of rich red plant groups, while pale pink and white forms provide softer colouring with pale blue lobelia and grey foliage.

Tuberous begonias make spectacular accents in window boxes or large pots, as do pendulous forms. The multiflora begonias are less dumpy than fibrous begonias and have the wide colour range of tuberous begonias without their rain-susceptible flowers. The pale yellow and peach coloured hybrids are perfect with pale blue violas or lobelia.

DAHLIA hybrids

H:20–180cm/8–72in   S:20–90cm/8–36in
The thousands of varieties of dahlias may be grown as half-hardy annuals, as hardy annuals or nearly-hardy herbaceous perennials on light, warm soils, or as tender perennials. However, the widest range of useful varieties are best treated as tender perennials, overwintered as tuberous roots dug out of the border after the first frosts, started into growth in early spring and propagated by rooting the young shoots.

Particularly useful are the elegant semi-cactus varieties of intermediate height: white, yellow, soft and bright orange, scarlet, crimson, lavender and purple. Many of the dark reds have the additional asset of dark coppery foliage.

HELIOTROPIUM peruvianum

Heliotrope, Cherry pie
H:45cm/18in   S:45cm/18in
Often raised from seed each year, heliotrope may be overwintered in pots to flower much earlier in the following summer on large plants. It has a subtle charm with dark foliage almost concealed beneath wide heads of white, lavender or deep purple flowers that have the delicious scent of cherry pie filling. The dark forms look good with hardy fuchsias of equally rich colour, or with pale pink fuchsias, begonias, or antirrhinums.

OSTEOSPERMUM jucundum

H:30cm/12in   S:45cm/18in
From a wide-spreading mound of narrow, soft green foliage, osteospermum (also known as *Dimorphotheca barberiae*) produces a constant succession of long-stemmed and long-petalled daisies of white, pink, pale purple or cream, often veined with blue around a darker blue eye. They need well-drained soil and full sun and are overwintered as rooted cuttings.

PELARGONIUM × hortorum

Zonal pelargonium, Geranium
H:45cm/18in   S:45cm/18in
Normally used in brilliantly coloured bedding schemes, these plants offer many more subtle possibilities: white varieties with sweet alyssum and grey foliage, soft orange with pale blue lobelia, pink with lavender petunias, etc.

Modern varieties are grown from seed as half-hardy annuals. The many variegated, dwarf and double varieties are easily propagated from cuttings. Particularly useful are 'Chelsea Gem' with white-edged leaves and pale salmon flowers, 'Mrs Henry Cox' with cream, red, purple and green markings on the leaf and salmon flowers, 'Harry Heiover' with a clear yellow leaf and scarlet flowers and 'Vesuvius', a miniature with almost black leaves and deep scarlet flowers.

SALVIA species

H:45–120cm/18–48in   S:45cm/18in
Salvias range from the hardy sage to the scarlet bedding salvia but many species are best regarded as tender perennials, propagated from cuttings in late summer.

Salvia farinacea has slender, deep purple-

Salvia patens 'Cambridge Blue'

blue spikes over grey-green foliage. Grown from seed or cuttings, it associates well with pink and white flowers and with grey foliage, lending a useful vertical accent. *S. guaranitica* is similar in habit but darker green with small spikes of clear, pale blue held above the foliage. It forms a handsome clump in the border and can be overwintered as divisions or rooted cuttings. *S. patens,* with large, brilliant blue flowers on loose spikes over bright green foliage can be grown from seed or from overwintered tubers. *S. fulgens* makes an even leafier plant with bright crimson flowers covered in a remarkable velvet

pile, wonderful with other red flowers and purple foliage. *S. rutilans* has orange-scarlet flowers in autumn on a wide-spreading bush of soft leaves that smell of pineapple when crushed. It is worth growing in a pot or in a sheltered border against a wall with *Eccremocarpus scaber* and brilliant blue *Ceratostigma willmottianum.*

VERBENA × hybrida

H:25cm/10in   S:45cm/18in

The several species of verbena and the more widely used hybrids make wide-spreading cushions of attractively toothed pale green leaves covered in late summer

and autumn with dense, rounded heads of five-petalled flowers. The colour range includes white, pink, lavender and purple, deep crimson, bright scarlet and vivid magenta, many of the hybrids having sparkling white centres. Verbenas are increasingly raised from seed as half-hardy annuals and there are good strains in pure colours and mixtures, but named varieties are still propagated by cuttings.

The loose trailing growth of the named varieties and the wide colour range make verbenas useful in the mixed border among roses, in pots and in bedding schemes.

BIENNIALS

Biennials are sown outside or, more commonly with expensive seed, under glass in summer and transplanted to nursery beds, being moved to their flowering positions in autumn to flower in the spring. A few, such as pansies and pinks may also be sown early under glass to flower later in the same year, treating them as half-hardy annuals.

CAMPANULA medium

Canterbury bell
H:75cm/30in   S:35cm/15in
Filling the gap between the burst of spring flowers and the gradual crescendo of late-summer annuals, Canterbury bells produce tall pyramids of large, bell-shaped flowers in pale and deep purple-blue, pink and white. The double forms, the so-called 'cup and saucer' varieties, are even more colourful with solid but delicate spires of closely-packed flowers. They associate particularly well with *Geranium ibericum*, which not only picks up the campanula colouring in its veined purple flowers but will also expand to cover the ground left by them when they die.

When there is room to raise stand-by plants in a nursery in the garden, Canterbury bells can be replaced by China asters or chrysanthemums.

CHEIRANTHUS cheiri

Wallflower
H:30–60cm/12–24in   S:25–45cm/10–18in
Loveliest of the spring bedding plants, wallflowers combine a range of beautiful colours with a marvellous fragrance. Old varieties, with flowers of deep red, orange or yellow, are traditionally combined with tall tulips. These warm colours also look wonderful among young red peony shoots or the emerging foliage of *Spiraea japonica* 'Goldflame'. Primrose wallflowers associate well with forget-me-not or with the

perennial *Brunnera macrophylla*, while the multicoloured blends of pink, buff, purple-red and cream may be combined with a broad edging of dark red or white double daisies or with bold bergenia foliage and the emerging shoots of purple berberis.

The brilliant orange Siberian wallflower, *Erysimum hieraciifolium*, is a startling colour in isolation but looks lovely with pale forget-me-nots.

DIGITALIS purpurea

Foxglove
H:1.5m/5ft   S:60cm/24in
'Excelsior' foxgloves with dense spikes of purple- or white-spotted tubular flowers all round the stem lack the grace of the wild species but, in the company of robust Canterbury bells, hummocks of sweet Williams and double daisies they contribute a feast of cottage-garden colour in early summer.

In the mixed border and among shrubs, the tall and gracefully arching one-sided spikes of the purple foxglove and its luminous white form are beyond compare. Both associate perfectly with old roses and the many plants that accompany old roses – geraniums, violas, dark sweet Williams and penstemons. Even lovelier among paler roses such as 'Penelope' is the soft apricot foxglove.

HESPERIS matronalis

Sweet rocket
H:75cm/30in   S:35cm/15in
This little-known but charming biennial produces fragrant white to deep lilac flowers in early summer. It will grow and flower in partial shade and on dry soil but, given good conditions, it will greatly exceed the dimensions indicated above.

Sweet rocket associates well with foxgloves and with honesty, which it resembles, or with the more compact domes of perennial wallflowers. Squeezed into a narrow border against a wall among a carpet of wallflowers, it creates a charming picture of fragrant informality.

LUNARIA annua

Honesty
H:60cm/24in   S:35cm/15in
Honesty does not transplant well and is best sown in the position in which it is to flower where it will provide interest for much of the year.

Emerging from a winter rosette of dark green foliage, the wide branching stems of honesty carry a succession of lilac or white flowers in early summer, followed by flat, rounded seed pods which may be dried for winter decoration. The species itself associates with lilacs, purple tulips and even the difficult colour of *Prunus* 'Sekiyama'. The white variegated form and the white flowered variety of this form excel in dark gardens and in the dry shade beneath trees and large shrubs, bringing light into these otherwise gloomy places.

MYOSOTIS alpestris

Forget-me-not
H:15cm/6in   S:15cm/6in
Although there are forget-me-nots with white or dusky pink flowers, their true glory lies in the clear sky blue and deeper blue varieties. These are lovely with pale or deep yellow tulips respectively, with orange and yellow wallflowers and with daffodils, whether in formal beds or informal drifts at the edge of a mixed border. The blues also associate well with white flowers, the double white arabis and mopheaded double daisies in particular, a combination which in turn provides a perfect setting for yellow or pink tulips or early peonies.

The pink and white forms provide a good foreground for honesty or sweet rocket and good companions for purple and red aubrieta.

ONOPORDUM acanthium

Scotch thistle
H:2.5m/8ft   S:1.5m/5ft

This spectacular plant emerges in late summer as a small, grey rosette, quickly expanding to form a large handsome plant 90cm/36in across with spiny-edged leaves of ghostly white. In the following spring and summer, while the basal leaves continue to grow, a central stem appears, extends and branches until it carries a wide candelabrum of small purple thistles. Apart from the thistle flowers, the whole plant is silver-grey and viciously spiny. It is very invasive if allowed to seed, and care needs to be taken that it does not overrun its neighbours.

Although the flowers are not remarkable, the skeleton that bears them aloft makes a spectacular focal point in the flower garden. It combines well with soft-coloured flowers such as diascias, penstemons, sidalceas and the grey-leaved *Fuchsia magellanica* 'Versicolor'.

VERBASCUM longifolium pannosum

Mullein
H:1.8m/6ft   S:90cm/36in

Another bold biennial, the giant mullein is as softly woolly as onopordum is spiny. For the largest, branching plants, seeds should be sown where they are to flower (or self-sown seedlings selected) and allowed to grow into large, grey rosettes. In the following summer the flower spike will emerge, densely covered in white wool, with small clusters of yellow flowers opening at intervals along the spike.

Despite its height, mullein is best grown towards the front of the border as an accent. Its grey rosettes blend well with other grey foliage of finer texture and the flowers associate both with the lavender and yellow flowers which many other grey-leaved plants produce.

Digitalis purpurea 'Excelsior Hybrids'

BULBS

Bulb catalogues contain a treasure trove of beautiful plants and, because bulbs carry their own store of food, they can be almost guaranteed to flower once even in very shady gardens. When buying bulbs, make sure they have been nursery-grown and not collected from the wild.

Spring bulbs provide a wonderful display of flowers at a time when few other plants have moved from their state of winter dormancy. On light soils and in informal situations, many of them can be planted deeply to avoid disturbance, and they will survive for many years. Some are robust enough to flourish in grass. It is important not to cut the grass until the bulb foliage has died away – delaying mowing until midsummer encourages wild flowers to follow on from the bulbs.

Summer-flowering bulbs also provide brilliant colour and many will push up through earlier flowering perennials, adding a useful vertical accent, while the autumn bulbs produce fresh, delicate flowers at a time when many plants in the flower garden are looking dishevelled.

ACIDANTHERA murielae

H:90cm/36in   S:15cm/6in
Acidanthera resembles a gladiolus, with its slender, swordlike leaves and tall spikes of flowers in late summer. The sweetly-scented flowers are white with a purple blotch at the base of each petal.

This graceful plant looks ideal in repeated small groups through the flower border or in large pots where it can be grown up through grey foliage, heliotrope, fuchsias and other rounded plants.

ALLIUM species

H:25–120cm/10–48in   S:10–30cm/4–12in
It is impossible to single out one allium for special consideration. They range from *A. karataviense* with densely globular heads of purple-pink flowers in late spring over almost flat, wide grey leaves to *A. siculum* (syn. *Nectaroscordum siculum*), a slender plant with loose heads of grey-green and dull purple flowers in late summer. Among the best are *A. christophii* with 15cm/6in globes of metallic purple-pink flowers in early summer, *A. giganteum* with dense 10cm/4in globes of bright lilac on stout 120cm/48in stems (also in early summer), *A. cernuum,* a slender plant with drooping, pale pink flowers on 25cm/10in stems later in the summer and *A. sphaerocephalon* with small, deep maroon heads of flowers on frail 45cm/18in stems

Allium giganteum

Cyclamen coum

in late summer or autumn. All are soft in their colouring, and are wonderful rising through purple or grey foliage or among perennial wallflowers, old roses and geraniums.

CHIONODOXA luciliae

Glory of the snow
H:15cm/6in   S:7cm/3in
Flowering in early spring with loose spikes of sky-blue flowers made even paler by a wide white band down each narrow petal, chionodoxa is lovely with primroses, the deeper blue scillas and late snowdrops. They will grow in grass and are equally suitable for the mixed border, planted in wide drifts among shrubs and the more permanent herbaceous plants where they will not be disturbed by cultivation.

Fritillaria meleagris 'Adonis'

COLCHICUM speciosum

Autumn crocus
H:25cm/10in   S:30cm/12in
There are many species of colchicum but *C. speciosum,* in various shades of purple-pink, and its lovely white form are easy and attractive. Flowers emerge before the leaves in early autumn and are easily broken down by heavy rain so they are best grown in grass or among low herbaceous plants for support. Hellebores, bergenias and *Penstemon heterophyllus* are good companions.

CROCUS tommasinianus

H:10cm/4in   S:5cm/2in
Crocus are almost synonymous with spring and *C. tommasinianus,* with its slender purple, lilac or occasionally white flowers opening almost flat in spring sunshine captures the charm of the genus as a whole. In the flower border it can increase so freely by offsets and seed that it is best confined to the ground beneath deciduous shrubs and to planting in grass.

There are many other species of crocus with flowers of purple, white, silvery lilac and yellow in addition to the better known large Dutch hybrids, providing a wonderful show from late winter into spring. *C. speciosus* and its white form flower in autumn, more delicately than the large colchicums, while *C. laevigatus* 'Fontaneyi' with delicately feathered flowers of deep and light purple and a delightful scent will flower throughout the winter if given a well-drained situation in full sun.

CYCLAMEN species

H:10cm/4in   S:20cm/8in
Cyclamen hederifolium (C. neapolitanum) is the best known of the hardy cyclamen, producing its pink or white twisted-petalled flowers in autumn just before the beautifully marbled leaves which then persist through winter, spring and early summer. It grows well beneath conifers and in dry, shady situations where little else will thrive and where its flowers light up the

darkness, but it is also useful in the rock garden, in raised beds and at the front of the border. Low purple sedums or ajuga provide a perfect setting.

Cyclamen coum has smaller but delightful rosy purple flowers through the depths of winter over dark green leaves with purple undersides; *C. repandum* follows in spring with tall and elegant magenta flowers.

ERANTHIS hyemalis

Winter aconite
H:10cm/4in   S:5cm/2in
The sharp yellow cups of winter aconite pushing through melted snow at the end of winter are a cheering sight. They grow best on alkaline soils and will grow well in dry shade, making extensive carpets beneath beech and other trees. Seed is the easiest form of increase as dried tubers do not always establish well, but the clumps may also be lifted and divided while still green after flowering.

Aconites do not grow well in grass but are lovely under shrubs and in large drifts through mixed borders. In the small garden their yellow flowers and longer lasting bright green ruffs are charming among peonies, geraniums and other herbaceous plants which will soon grow to cover the dying foliage of the aconites.

FRITILLARIA species

H:100cm/40in   S:30cm/12in
Fritillaria imperialis (crown imperial) is among the most striking of the early summer bulbs, producing stout, pale green shoots in spring that grow rapidly until they are topped by a crown of yellow, orange or brick red pendant flowers and a final rosette of leaves. The leaves quickly die away after flowering but on fairly heavy alkaline soil the bulbs form large, long-lived clumps and make a distinctive contribution to the flower border. The whole plant has a strong foxy odour, unpleasant in an enclosed garden.

Fritillaria meleagris, the graceful snake's head fritillary, with a single, large nodding bell at the end of each frail stem, poses no such problem. It grows especially well on wet soils but will tolerate dry. The white form, 'Adonis', is even more beautiful than the intriguing chequered flower of the species.

GALANTHUS nivalis

Snowdrop
H:15cm/6in   S:7cm/3in
The charm of the snowdrop is almost greater when a single clump shines from a dark corner in a small garden in late winter, showing each crystalline pendant to perfection, than when great sheets of nodding flowers spread over the woodland floor. The grey-green leaves are also a great asset, setting the flowers off and then growing to form arching mounds later in spring. The possibilities for using snowdrops are endless: among low herbaceous plants, under deciduous shrubs, or among ferns and low evergreens.

GLADIOLUS hybrids

H:75–120cm/30–48in   S:20–30cm/8–12in
With their sword-shaped leaves and tall spikes of flowers in a wide range of soft and brilliant colours, gladioli are wonderful plants to use as vertical accents. Tall, large-flowered hybrids need staking but the lighter primulinus, butterfly and nanus hybrids, shorter and with more elegantly tapered spikes, will usually stand on their own. Each spike lasts for several weeks but the season can be extended by planting groups at 10 to 14 day intervals from early spring to early summer.

HYACINTHUS orientalis

Hyacinth
H:25cm/10in   S:20cm/8in
The cultivated hybrids of hyacinth have heavy spikes of fragrant flowers in white,

pink, blue, red, purple, pale yellow and apricot-orange. The soft colours, heavy fragrance and solid, uniform flower spikes have long made them favourite plants for spring bedding, either alone or with an edging of forget-me-not or double daisy. As pot plants they are easily forced to flower during the winter.

They are equally useful in the informal flower garden. On well-drained soils the bulbs will last for many years and, after the first year, the flower spikes become less tightly packed and more graceful. Their early flowering makes them invaluable in the mixed border.

IRIS reticulata

H:20cm/8in   S:5cm/2in

When their leaves have barely emerged from the soil, the flowers, clear violet blue, sky blue or deep maroon with yellow markings within, open quickly on warm days in early spring to release their wonderful scent and to delight early bees. On light soil they quickly increase and it is worth dividing congested clumps every three or four years to enjoy the shape of the individual flowers. The long, slender leaves which emerge after flowering become untidy as they die away but this is a small price to pay for the flowers.

It is easily grown in pots, either to bring into the house or to use in strategic positions in the garden.

LILIUM species and hybrids

Lilies

H:60–120cm/24–48in   S:25–45cm/ 10–18in

The range of easily grown hybrid lilies has increased enormously in recent years and the price of individual bulbs has dropped so these aristocrats of the bulb world should find a place in every garden. Species such as *LL. auratum, pardalinum, speciosum* and *lancifolium* on acid soils, or

LEFT *Galanthus nivalis, Eranthis hyemalis*
RIGHT *Lilium* Asiatic Hybrids

LL. candidum, chalcedonicum, henryi, marta-gon and *regale* on alkaline soils offer a range of height, season, colour and beautiful forms of flower for sun or partial shade and most are intensely fragrant. The Asiatic hybrids and (on acid soils only) the trumpet-shaped Oriental hybrids offer a still wider range and are very inexpensive.

Most lilies thrive among other plants which shade the soil and support their wide-branching flower stems. The late-flowering hybrids are invaluable for growing through herbaceous plants which have finished flowering.

NARCISSUS hybrids

Daffodil and narcissus
H:15–45cm/6–18in   S:7–15cm/3–6in
The long trumpets and radiating petals of the bright yellow daffodils are an indication that winter is really over. They create beautiful pictures with yellow forsythia, blue scillas and brunnera, early white cherries, magnolias and amelanchiers and golden young leaves. *Narcissus bulbocodium* and the charming dwarf cyclamineus hybrids flower very early and will often last well: 'Tête à Tête' in particular will often flower for six weeks. Juncifolius hybrids

such as the tall but slender 'Trevithian' have a wonderful scent while 'Beersheba' and other white daffodils have an ethereal beauty. Last to flower is the very old *poeticus* 'Old Pheasants Eye' (syn. *N.p. recurva*), with broad white petals, a small bright red cup and, again, a wonderful scent.

The large daffodils are best used in large drifts in grass as they are untidy after flowering but the smaller hybrids are useful in the smallest garden among herbaceous plants that will conceal their dying foliage.

NERINE bowdenii

H:45cm/18in   S:15cm/6in

Left undisturbed against the foot of a sunny wall *N. bowdenii* will build up into large clumps of bulbs with glossy, strap-shaped leaves in early summer dying away before the large clear-pink flowers appear in profusion. They are lovely with low grey foliage and with ceratostigma, caryopteris and other blue or grey-blue flowers but care must be taken not to shade the nerine bulbs as this will severely impair their flowering.

Related to nerine are three other plants that deserve a mention: *Sternbergia lutea,* which looks like a robust golden crocus, the white *Zephyranthes candida* and the pink *Z. grandiflora* with wide, starlike flowers. All flower most freely in narrow, sunny borders in the autumn.

SCILLA species

H:15cm/6in   S:7cm/3in

The intense blue of *S. bifolia* and the slightly later *S. siberica* are very well known but *S. tubergeniana* (syn. *S. mischtschenkoana*) is surprisingly neglected. It opens its ice-blue flowers at ground level in late winter and the spike slowly expands to its full height over about six weeks. It is one of the loveliest and longest lasting of all the spring bulbs.

TIGRIDIA pavonia

Tiger flower
H:45cm/18in   S:12cm/5in

Tigridias may be planted into the garden in sheltered situations but much better results are obtained by planting them quite thickly, 10 or 12 in a 15cm/6in pot, to bring out when in flower. With successive plantings through spring and early summer they will flower from late summer into autumn and can then be gradually dried off to store over winter. The shoots are rather fragile and staking each pot with

LEFT *Narcissus bulbocodium conspicuus*
RIGHT *Tulipa clusiana*

a few split canes and string is usually worthwhile.

The reward will be a succession of exotic flowers, each with three round petals of pink, red, orange or yellow and a cup-shaped white centre heavily spotted with dark brown, over a period of two or three weeks. They can be associated with grey foliage or with small-flowered plants such as verbena or lobelia but they are spectacular enough to stand alone on a terrace or other strategic position.

TULIPA hybrids

Tulip
H:15–90cm/6–36in   S:15cm/6in

There is no flower with a wider colour range than the tulip and, with a season extending from early spring with the dwarf kaufmanniana and greigii hybrids to early summer for the tall darwins and cottage tulips, they have enormous value in the flower garden. Traditionally they are used with wallflowers, aubrieta, polyanthus or violas, either formally or in irregular drifts in the mixed border. They are also lovely, in similar combinations, in pots, especially as this lifts the scented but short 'General de Wet' (orange) and 'Bellona' (yellow) nearer the nose.

On light soils tulips may be planted deeply (20–25cm/8–10in) and they will survive for many years among herbaceous plants. White, yellow, pink or orange tulips look wonderful over a carpet of brunnera; red and purple tulips harmonize with the young purple foliage of fennel, peonies, cotinus or *Heuchera americana.*

HERBACEOUS PERENNIALS

Typically, herbaceous perennials die back to resting buds at ground level in the autumn and produce a new top in spring and summer. New unfurling shoots are a major asset in the flower garden, followed by the flowers themselves and often attractive seed heads.

It is a very versatile group of plants. Some are excellent ground covers, some harmonize with early bulbs then cover their dying leaves, some will flower for a very long season while others have a fleeting but glorious contribution to make. The dead foliage of some herbaceous plants remains attractive throughout the winter while others are truly evergreen. A few produce their precious flowers in the depths of winter.

ACHILLEA 'Moonshine'

H:45cm/18in   S:45cm/18in

This is a soft-coloured plant with sprays of finely dissected grey-green leaves topped in summer by flat heads of lemon yellow flowers. It flowers over a long period and remains attractive for a long time, fading gradually to light brown.

It will not tolerate poorly drained soil and needs frequent division to keep it compact and vigorous but is otherwise a trouble-free plant, ideal for the edge of the border where its long-stemmed flowers can arch forward among blue agapanthus or purple salvias.

A. filipendulina produces deeper yellow flower heads on a taller plant.

AGAPANTHUS 'Headbourne Hybrids'

H:60–90cm/24–36in   S:45cm/18in

Most of the South African blue lilies are not hardy although they make spectacular plants in containers for summer display, but the Headbourne hybrids are excellent garden plants with upright clumps of bright green narrow leaves and globes of clear blue or white flowers on long stems well above the leaves in late summer and autumn. The seed heads, too, are attractive and can be left standing into the winter. There are named varieties varying in height and intensity of flower colour but all are trouble-free, long-lived plants forming dense clumps. They are easily propagated by division in spring and worth using in large drifts or as small accents of bright blue.

ALSTROEMERIA 'Ligtu Hybrids'

Peruvian lily
H:90cm/36in   S:90cm/36in

Alstroemerias require a well-drained soil in full sun and are difficult to establish initially so are best planted as clumps of seedlings from pots. However, once

established, they will thrive without attention for many years, spreading vigorously underground to form wide masses of spectacular flowers in summer over delightful pale grey-green foliage. Wide heads of delicate pink, yellow, white, orange or lilac flowers are heavily spotted with dark purple.

ALTHAEA rosea

Hollyhock
H:2.5m/8ft   S:75cm/30in
Tall spires of hollyhocks are almost synonymous with cottage gardens. Sadly the ravages of hollyhock rust mean that it is not a long-lived plant, but seed may be sown early in the spring under glass to flower in late summer and autumn or sown in summer to flower earlier and on taller spikes in the following year.

Most varieties produce double flowers, longer lasting and more colourful than singles but giving the shorter spikes of annually raised plants a rather dumpy character. The colour range is very wide – white, yellow, red, pink and purple – and the flowers appear above large rosettes of soft green leaves.

ANCHUSA azurea

H:90cm/36in   S:75cm/30in
Anchusa is a short-lived perennial, only suitable for well-drained and preferably alkaline soils, but worn out plants are easily replaced by root cuttings taken in autumn. From a basal rosette of coarse, bristly leaves it produces a wide spreading spire of small, brilliant blue flowers for a month or more in early summer. The flower head is robust but inclined to keel over at ground level so a short stake is advisable. There are several named varieties including 'Loddon Royalist', a rich, deep blue, and 'Opal', light blue.

LEFT *Achillea* 'Moonshine'
RIGHT *Anchusa azurea*

ANEMONE × hybrida

Japanese anemone
H:1.2m/4ft   S:60cm/24in
These are among the most beautiful plants for the autumn flower garden, with long, slender stems carrying branching heads of white, pale or deep pink flowers high above the 40cm/15in mounds of hand-some leaves. The widely-spaced round flowers, each with a yellow tuft of stamens in the centre, make a useful contrast to the mistier clouds of buddlejas, Michaelmas daisies and other autumn flowers, and Japanese anemone is hardy enough to flourish almost anywhere on well-drained soil. It is lovely in long drifts rising through borders of earlier flowering shrubs or through carpets of ground-covering geraniums and excellent towards the front of herbaceous borders where its low foliage creates a good edge while the tall flower stems provide height without obscuring the border.

AQUILEGIA hybrids

Columbine
H:90cm/36in   S:35cm/15in
The long-spurred flowers of aquilegia dancing on tall straight stems above mounds of elegant glaucous foliage give an exuberance to the early summer flower garden. If dead flowers are removed the season will be extended and, when the flowers are finished, it is easy to remove the stiff stems at the base, leaving the foliage as an excellent foil for later flowers in the border. Its colour range is wide, from white, cream and pale pink through lavender to bright yellow or red, often in bicolour combinations from soft lemon and white to bright red and yellow. It is easily raised from seed and, if planted out into a nursery for the first flowering season (or grown in pots in the smaller garden), the best colours for particular situations can be labelled and moved in the autumn to their permanent positions.

ASTER × frikartii

H:75cm/30in   S:45cm/18in
The Michaelmas daisies (referring strictly only to *Aster novi-belgii*) are the mainstay of the autumn flower garden but are prone to mildew and subject to attack from tarsonemid mites which destroy the flower buds. *A. × frikartii* does not suffer from these problems and its flowers, long-rayed daisies of lavender-blue, are produced over a long period in summer and autumn on strong, upright stems. It requires a good soil and a sunny position to give of its best and, like many long-flowering plants, needs regular division to keep it vigorous, but it amply repays these efforts.

There are many other lovely asters, including *A. acris* 'Nana' (syn. *A. sedifolius nanus*) with domes of pale flowers over grey foliage in late summer, *A. divaricatus* with tiny white stars on almost black stems in autumn and the intriguing *A. lateriflorus* 'Horizontalis' with small lilac flowers in dense horizontal sprays over purple-tinted foliage in late autumn.

ASTRANTIA major

H:60cm/24in   S:60cm/24in
Although astrantia will survive on dry soils it is at its best on a good, moist soil. It will then produce mounds of deeply toothed, dark green foliage with a long display of flowers through summer and autumn. The flowers are unusual hemi-spheres of feathery stamens (in fact tiny flowers) within a ruff of greenish white bracts. In the variety 'Shaggy', the bracts are long, slightly twisted and divided at the tips, while 'Rubra' is a deep purple-pink. None are brilliantly colourful plants but the freedom with which their fascinat-ing flowers are produced, even in shade, make them invaluable on moist soils.

FAR LEFT *Anemone × hybrida* 'Honorine Jobert'
LEFT *Brunnera macrophylla*
RIGHT *Campanula lactiflora*

BRUNNERA macrophylla

H:45cm/18in   S:45cm/18in

The soft-green heart-shaped leaves of brunnera are semi-evergreen and provide useful foliage in the foreground of the flower border during the winter but it is worth shearing them off in late winter so that the new flower stems, with pale blue forget-me-not flowers in airy panicles, are visible from the moment they appear. The flower stems continue to extend for a month or more in spring but gradually disappear as they fade into an increasing mound of attractive foliage. Brunnera is lovely interplanted with white daffodils or the pale *Narcissus triandrus* hybrids with which it harmonizes perfectly before growing to hide their dying foliage.

CAMPANULA lactiflora

Bellflower

H:1.5m/5ft   S:1m/3ft

Campanulas range from low alpines to border giants, encompassing many useful plants for the flower garden, but *C. lactiflora* is one of the most beautiful. Long dark green leaves, grey-green beneath, are borne on tall, straight stems terminated in midsummer by large domes of flower in various shades of lavender-purple or white. If the main flower head is removed when it fades, smaller lateral spikes will continue the display for many weeks. The plant is usually self-supporting but it is worth staking to ensure against damage from heavy rain.

This is lovely with shrub roses or with the yellow flowers of day-lilies and is robust enough to support later-flowering clematis.

CENTAUREA ruthenica

Knapweed
H:75cm/30in   S:45cm/18in
Blue is the colour usually associated with the knapweeds but this species has fluffy flowers of a delightful pale lemon on long, dark green stems over deeply toothed dark green foliage. The whole plant is very slender and lovely with blue, purple or white companions. It thrives on well-drained soils.

CENTRANTHUS ruber

Valerian
H:60cm/24in   S:60cm/24in
Valerian grows naturally on limestone cliffs and looks wonderful springing out of cracks in the rock with rounded masses of fleshy, grey-green foliage and heads of small pink flowers. In the garden it creates a similar atmosphere of profusion. The very dark form *C.r. atrococcineus* is lovely with purple foliage and old roses and there is an even more attractive white form ideal for the white garden or with blue, pale yellow, pink and other soft-coloured flowers. It flowers repeatedly throughout the summer and, when it starts to look bedraggled, may be cut to the ground to encourage a new crop of foliage with a few late flowers.

CEPHALARIA gigantea

H:2m/7ft   S:1m/3ft
A close relative of scabious, *Cephalaria gigantea,* also known as *C. tatarica,* has large but elegant flowers of pale lemon on wide-branched stems over handsome rosettes of toothed, dark green leaves in early summer. In colour it closely resembles *Centaurea ruthenica* but it is a much larger plant suitable only for large gardens where it creates a splendid effect among blue iris or with lupins.

Centranthus ruber atrococcineus

CERATOSTIGMA plumbaginoides

H:25cm/10in S:35cm/15in

This semi-evergreen trailing plant is invasive on light soils but makes an excellent ground cover of soft green leaves at the front of a sunny border. In autumn the leaves turn rich maroon, a signal for the plant to produce its brilliant blue flowers, which it will do until the frost. It is lovely among fuchsias and with grey-leaved plants and, if sheared off at ground level in late winter, will leave the ground vacant for scillas, crocus and other early bulbs before growing to hide their dying foliage with its own new leaves.

C. willmottianum (H:60cm/24in S:60cm/24in) is similar in flower and in flowering season but grows as an upright bush of grey-green leaves. It is usually killed to the ground in cold winters but it is worth waiting until spring to cut off the dead stems for the sake of the mound of warm brown seed heads. In sheltered gardens it will grow into a larger sub-shrub.

CHRYSANTHEMUM maximum

Shasta daisy
H:90cm/36in S:60cm/24in

An unstinting supply of large white daisies will fill the gap which occurs in the flower border between the glory of early summer and the profusion of asters, goldenrods and hybrid chrysanthemums in the autumn. The flowers may be single, with clear yellow centres, mop-headed doubles or anemone-centred with a collar of long petals around a compact dome of smaller florets. Most need staking with twiggy brushwood unless they can be allowed to lean on adjacent plants.

There are many other chrysanthemums, not least the highly developed hybrids in hundreds of varieties, but these have been bred mainly for exhibition and cut-flower use and few make reliable garden plants. Where they can be protected over winter, cuttings rooted in spring and planted out after frost, they are very beautiful and useful plants.

Coreopsis verticillata

COREOPSIS verticillata

H:60cm/24in S:45cm/18in

The very bright yellow of these narrow-petalled daisies is set in a mist of finely divided bright green foliage so the effect is cheerful but never garish. It flowers for several months through the summer and early autumn and spreads steadily but not invasively into wide clumps. Recently a sulphur yellow variety, 'Moonbeam', has been introduced, a wonderful plant to associate with the many lavender-purple flowers of late summer.

CORYDALIS ochroleuca

H:20cm/8in S:30cm/12in

With tufts of ferny, pale green foliage and a habit of seeding itself into cracks and crevices, this is a charming plant for blurring the edges of the flower garden. It tolerates shade and dry soils, especially if the roots can extend under paving, and it can become invasive on heavy, wet soils although it is easily pulled up. The tubular flowers are milk-white, with yellow markings around the tight-lipped mouth and are borne in great profusion in spring, then intermittently through summer and autumn. C. lutea is identical except for its yellow flowers. Both are lovely with blue flowers or grey foliage.

CRAMBE cordifolia

H:2m/7ft S:1.5m/5ft

This extraordinary plant will produce mounds of dark green, crumpled cabbage leaves in spring with stout flower stems arising from the middle of each crown in early summer. These dissipate into a wide cloud of tiny white flowers, honey-scented but tainted, if picked, by the strong cabbage smell of the plant. The stems continue to create an effect after flowering but will eventually collapse and should then be removed. The contrast between the coarse leaves and tiny flowers is spectacular and room should be found for this in any reasonably drained garden.

CROCOSMIA × crocosmiiflora

Montbretia
H:45cm/18in   S:30cm/12in
Sheaves of grassy foliage and slender
arching spikes of orange flowers in late
summer or early autumn endow the
montbretias with great charm. The hardiest ones will spread into crowded colonies
with few flowers unless divided frequently. Many old hybrids are less vigorous
plants and may not increase at all unless
given a rich, moist soil in a warm,
sheltered situation. However, the pale
apricot 'Solfatare' with bronze leaves,
brick-red and yellow 'Jackanapes' and
other hybrids are worth this trouble.

Crocosmia masonorum and the Bressing-
ham hybrids between it and C. paniculata
(syn. Curtonus paniculatus) are much taller
and more vigorous plants with broad
arching leaves and towering spikes of
glowing orange-red. They make excellent
focal points in the border.

DIASCIA cordifolia

H:15cm/6in   S:20cm/8in
The diascias have only recently found their
way into cultivation but are already very
popular. None are reliably hardy, especially in a wet winter, but they will thrive in a
warm, well-drained soil and are easily
propagated from cuttings. D. cordifolia is
the lowest of the several species, a close
mat of small glaucous grey-green leaves
only 2.5cm/1in high topped by slender
stems carrying a long succession of delicate salmon-pink flowers with a darker
eye. It is lovely as an edging plant,
especially where it can extend out into
gaps in the path. D. rigescens is much taller
(40cm/15in or more), with longer spikes
of flower, charming with the solid globes
of agapanthus or among the heavier blue
spikes of Penstemon heterophyllus.

DICENTRA formosa

H:35cm/15in   S:45cm/18in
A fleshy plant with finely divided, ferny
leaves, dicentra produces sprays of dang-
ling pink lockets above the mounds of
foliage in spring and early summer. It is an
undemanding plant but the flower season
is much extended in a moist soil. D. f.
oregana is closely related and the white
form of this is exceptionally beautiful,
with bronze-flushed grey leaves and warm
white flowers.

Dicentra spectabilis is a much taller plant
with large pendant flowers on arching
stems. It and its white form are very
beautiful but will only grow in a very
moist, rich soil and with frequent division.

DIERAMA pulcherrimum

Angel's fishing rod
H:1.2m/4ft   S:75cm/30in
Although tall, this is an immensely graceful plant with narrow grassy foliage and,
in late summer, long arching sprays of
narrow funnel-shaped flowers in pink or
purple. The wiry stems sway in the wind
and the effect continues to be attractive
when the flowers have been replaced by
the round brown beads of the seed heads.
They grow best in a moist soil in sun, but
will tolerate drier conditions. Despite their
height, they should be grown near the
front of the border to appreciate their
lovely silhouette.

DORONICUM columnae (syn. D. cordatum)

Leopard's bane
H:35cm/15in   S:20cm/8in
Flowering in spring, doronicum has narrow petalled daisies of sharp yellow borne
above neat mats of dark green heart-
shaped leaves. The season is quite short
but this is a lovely plant for bringing
spring gaiety to the front of the border. It
will spread into wide mats if it is divided
after flowering and replanted in fresh soil.

Doronicum columnae

D. plantagineum 'Excelsium' is a later-flowering and much larger plant producing branching heads of widely spaced large flowers in spring and early summer, reaching 75cm/30in or more.

EUPHORBIA species

H:45cm/18in S:60cm/24in
Of the many handsome euphorbias *E. polychroma* (syn. *E. epithymoides*) is one of the brightest. Truly herbaceous, it emerges in spring as a tuft of brilliant yellow bracts surrounding the insignificant flowers, vying with daffodils, forsythia and doronicums in colour. The colour slowly fades until, by midsummer, it is a wide mound of grey-green leaves. There is also a bronze-leaved form.

E. griffithii is a taller plant (H:75cm/30in; S:60cm/24in). Rosettes of bright orange bracts emerge in spring and extend on upright stems which are eventually clothed with dark grey-green leaves.

GERANIUM wallichianum

Crane's bill
H:40cm/15in S:75cm/30in
Among many beautiful geraniums, *G. wallichianum* excels because of its late and long flowering season and its pale blue, white-eyed flowers. The foliage is attractive early in the year – mounds of soft grey green with darker spots at the base of the veins. In late summer the mound spills over and the plant produces trailing flower stems that insert themselves among other plants in the border. It is excellent among roses, trailing over grey-leaved plants and among late achilleas and potentillas.

GEUM species and hybrids

H:30–45cm/12–18in S:25cm/10in
Geum 'Borisii' (syn. *G. borisii × montanum*) starts the season in late spring with slender, branching sprays of small round flowers of a very bright orange above neat rosettes of lobed, deep green leaves. Associated with the paler copper-yellow *G.* 'Georgenberg', either in distinct

Geum 'Borisii'

groups or in a mixture, the result is a glowing warmth. *G. chiloense* follows in early summer with fewer but larger flowers, each with charming wavy-edged petals on nodding stalks well above the leaves. 'Lady Stratheden' is a soft yellow and 'Mrs Bradshaw' a bright orange-scarlet. Given good soil and frequent division, both varieties will flower into autumn after the first main flush of flower.

GYPSOPHILA paniculata

H:1m/3ft S:1.2m/4ft
Gertrude Jekyll described gypsophila as a 'cloud of white blossom settled down on the flower border'. It needs some support and will only flourish on a well-drained, alkaline soil. Given this it is a long-lived plant and its grey stems, appearing late in the spring, are useful for concealing the remains of oriental poppies and early bulbs, doubly earning its space in the border. It flowers in mid to late summer, then fades to a pleasant straw brown.

HELENIUM autumnale

H:90cm/36in S:60cm/24in
The named hybrids between *H. autumnale* and closely related species provide glowing colour in the border in late summer and autumn. Wide-petalled daisies literally cover the plant and colours range from deep yellow through various degrees of copper tinting to deep maroon. Petals and leaves are prone to wilt on dry soils but they are otherwise undemanding plants. Their rounded form makes them excellent mixers but they need the company of kniphofias, tall grasses or coppery-leaved shrubs to avoid monotony.

HELLEBORUS orientalis

Lenten rose
H:30cm/12in S:60cm/24in
Among the most beautiful of all winter-flowering plants, the Lenten roses range in colour from greenish white, blush and deep pink heavily spotted with maroon to deep plum-purples which verge on black.

The flower season extends from mid-winter, with flowers unfurling from ground level, into early summer when the flowers shed their seeds. Hellebores are reliably evergreen but, as the old foliage becomes tattered by the time the flowers are at their best, it is wise to cut off the old foliage in early winter.

Hellebores are hardy and long-lived, especially on alkaline soils, and will grow in the shade of trees or buildings. They are lovely in large drifts under winter-flowering shrubs.

HEMEROCALLIS hybrids

Day-lilies
H:45–120cm/18–48in   S:45–120cm/18–48in
The attraction of day-lilies begins in early spring when the new foliage pushes through the bare soil, ahead of most other herbaceous plants, forming fans of bright yellow-green – a perfect setting for many spring bulbs. The flower season begins in late spring with the low-growing *H. dumortieri* and extends into autumn with

the tall but slender flowers of *H. multiflora*. Innumerable hybrids span the summer season with colours ranging from pale lemon, almost ivory, through deeper yellow to orange and deep red. There are also several pink and apricot hybrids, some with frilled or striped petals. Some of the modern hybrids are too heavy to stand up well in a wet summer but many are first-class garden plants, lovely with delphiniums or geraniums, and good weed smotherers for the large garden. The white-variegated form of *H. fulva* 'Flore Pleno' creates a stunning effect with its spring foliage.

HOSTA species and hybrids

H:60cm/24in   S:60cm/24in
Grown primarily as foliage plants all hostas have flowers, some of which are exceedingly beautiful. Most tolerate a range of soil types and situations but flourish on moist soil in partial shade.

Hosta lancifolia has narrow dark green leaves with lilac flower spikes in early autumn, and is quite tolerant of dry soil.

H. sieboldiana is the most dramatic with huge waxy grey leaves but the flowers tend to remain hidden among the leaves. *H. plantaginea* is the loveliest in flower with tall spires of large white and heavily fragrant flowers produced over pale green glossy leaves in autumn. The various forms of *H. fortunei* also combine beauty of flowers and foliage, especially *H.f.* 'Albopicta' with yellow and soft green variegated leaves and lilac flowers in slender spikes in late summer.

IRIS × germanica

Flag iris
H:90–120cm/36–48in   S:45cm/18in
There are more than two hundred species of iris, some growing well in very dry, sunny situations, others perfectly at home in shallow water. The bearded flag iris is best on a fertile but well-drained soil. It has flat fans of grey-green swordlike foliage and tall, more or less branched stems with large flowers in early summer. Iris encompasses the widest colour range of all border plants: white, pale and deep yellow, pink and brown, orange, blue and purple, often with contrasting beards or in bicoloured combinations. Blue varieties are usually sweetly scented.

After flowering, the plants soon become unsightly but this may be countered by sowing slender annuals among the rhizomes to flower later in the summer, taking care not to shade the iris too heavily or they will rot.

KNAUTIA macedonica

H:60cm/24in   S:45cm/18in
This charming and little-known plant thrives in well-drained soil in sun and flowers in late summer with pincushion flowers of an unusually deep crimson. It is lovely among purple foliage or with grey, and will add contrasting richness to pale blue agapanthus.

LEFT *Helleborus orientalis*
RIGHT *Knautia macedonica*

KNIPHOFIA triangularis

Red hot poker
H:75cm/30in   S:60cm/24in
Red hot pokers are usually thought of as large, often coarse plants with fat red and yellow spikes of flower but there are also several much more slender types derived from *K. triangularis* and its near relatives. *K. nelsonii* has glowing orange flowers over a fountain of grassy foliage in autumn and this is followed by *K. macowanii* with slightly smaller spikes. Both are wonderful against orange-red brick walls but stand out well, too, against white or grey walls, or among the blue flowers and autumn foliage of the ceratostigmas. 'Little Maid', *modesta,* 'Ice Queen' and 'Shining Sceptre' are other good, refined but emphatic varieties.

LIGULARIA dentata 'Desdemona'

H:90cm/36in   S:75cm/30in
With large, round leaves on long stalks, dark green above and rich maroon purple below, *L. dentata* 'Desdemona' is a hand-some plant from the moment it appears above ground in the spring. At this stage it is wonderful with red, deep purple or creamy white tulips. In midsummer sturdy flower stems emerge and unfold to carry aloft large mounds of deep yellow, rather ragged petalled daisies that continue to open until early autumn. The almost orange-yellow flowers against large, dark leaves are an arresting sight. *L. przewalskii* 'The Rocket', with smaller jagged-edged leaves and narrow upright spikes of brassy yellow flowers is an excellent companion to the rounded 'Desdemona'. Both need a good, moist soil and partial shade.

LIMONIUM latifolium

Sea lavender
H:45cm/18in   S:45cm/18in
A plant for well-drained soil in full sun, sea lavender has glossy, dark green leaves which it retains in winter, looking like a slim, elegant bergenia. The crown of leaves enlarges during the summer, small groups forming an effective feature at the edge of a border, and in late summer the flower spike emerges, with wiry stems carrying clouds of tiny, lavender-blue flowers. The flower spikes often bend at the base, causing them to rest on neighbouring plants or to spill over the edge of the border. Where this is not desired, use a short cane to anchor the base of the flower stem. Sea lavender is lovely with late diascias, penstemons and when resting on cushions of rue or other grey-leaved plants.

OENOTHERA species

Evening primrose
H:25cm/10in   S:60cm/24in
There are many good evening primroses, the most colourful being the forms of *O. tetragona* such as 'Fireworks', an upright plant with a crown of red flower buds opening to provide a long succession of deep yellow flowers. *O. missouriensis* is a trailing species, which, on light soil, becomes a wide-spreading carpet of grey-green foliage supporting an array of large, soft yellow flowers unfurling from red-spotted buds through summer and much of the autumn. It is beautiful in front of the small-flowered potentillas, with the purple spikes of *Salvia farinacea* or the globes of blue agapanthus.

PAEONIA species and hybrids

H:60–120cm/24–48in   S:75–90cm/30–36in
Undoubtedly the most opulent inhabitants of the flower border, peonies have only a short flowering season. However, such is the beauty of their crimson-maroon young shoots, the breathtaking beauty of the flowers and the quality of their foliage for the rest of summer and autumn that their ephemerality must be excused. The plants themselves are long-lived.

P. lactiflora hybrids have large double or single flowers of white, blush pink, deep pink or deep maroon on tall stems and most are fragrant. They need staking except in the most sheltered situations.

Paeonia lactiflora 'Bowl of Beauty'

Paeonia mlokosewitschii

P. officinalis flowers early with huge double flowers of bright red, palest pink or white on lower, sturdier and usually self-supporting plants. Both provide a good foil and later cover for early bulbs and will support late-flowering clematis. There are many beautiful species, too, notably the pale yellow, single *P. mlokosewitschii.*

PAPAVER orientale

Oriental poppy
H:90cm/36in   S:90cm/36in
Bright orange, salmon pink, white or deep scarlet-crimson with black blotches at the base of their large, crumpled petals, the oriental poppies are gorgeous flowers for late spring. There are many good, old varieties and new varieties are being added. The one failing of these lovely flowers is that they die away early in the summer, leaving large gaps in the border. This is overcome by interplanting with green or purple fennel or gypsophila, or by planting out dahlias or other tender perennials, taking care not to damage the fleshy roots of the poppies.

PENSTEMON hybrids

H:45–90cm/18–36in   S:45cm/18in
There are many hardy or nearly hardy penstemons, producing slender spikes of tubular flowers freely in summer and autumn. *P. heterophyllus* is the hardiest with glaucous foliage, maroon-tinted in winter, and small spikes of lavender-blue flowers. 'Garnet', a magenta-crimson, and 'Sour Grapes', a subtle blend of green and purple, are useful among old roses and with grey foliage, while 'White Bedder', 'Apple Blossom', 'Evelyn', 'Schoenholz-eri' and 'Alice Hindley' provide a range from white to pink, red and pale lilac. All are best on well-drained soil in sun. Where hardiness is doubtful, cuttings will root easily for overwintering.

Papaver orientale 'Beauty of Livermere'

PHLOX paniculata

H:90cm/36in S:75cm/30in

The border phlox flower in late summer and autumn, with solid domes of neat flowers in white, pink, lavender, purple, red and near-orange. They have a heavy scent which some find attractive, others oppressive. On moist soils they are free flowering, long lasting and opulent. They will survive on drier soils, but the flowers drop quickly and the leaves often look dull and limp. Dead-heading when the flowers begin to fade will lead to a second flush of smaller clusters. Phlox start into growth early in the year. Most varieties have pale green foliage but some purple varieties have deep bronze foliage, lovely with yellow or white crocus and the deep yellow *Eranthis × tubergenii*.

PRIMULA × polyanthus

Polyanthus
H:25cm/10in S:25cm/10in

There are many beautiful species of primula, not least the very early drumstick primula, *P. denticulata*, the brilliantly colourful candelabra primulas so good on wet soils in late spring and the late-flowering, fragrant *P. florindae*. The polyanthus, however, has attracted the attention of plant breeders for many years and many lovely plants have been produced. The very large flowered hybrids are not long-lived in gardens, being suited mainly to pot plant production. The delightful laced polyanthus have neat gold rims outlining flowers of red, blue or purple and are best planted where each flower can be admired. The aristocrats of the polyanthus are the Barnhaven strains, in an enormous range of colours including grey-purples and browns in addition to the more normal reds, yellows and blues. The darker reds usually have bronze-tinted foliage, evergreen in winter, and are lovely for their early flower colour in the red border.

LEFT *Primula florindae, P. cockburniana*
RIGHT *Salvia × superba* 'East Friesland'

SALVIA × superba

H:45–75cm/18–30in S:45cm/18in

The various forms and hybrids of *S. nemorosa* and *S. pratensis* now included in *S. × superba* have spikes of lavender-purple flowers of varying shades surrounded by much longer lasting bracts of similar colouring. 'May Night' ('Mainacht') is the earliest, with 'Lubeca', 'East Friesland' and 'Superba' taller and later, continuing into late summer. The upright stems clad with rough grey-green leaves are attractive, harmonizing well with grey or purple foliage, with old roses, and with pale yellow achilleas, evening primroses or kniphofias.

SCABIOSA caucasica

H:75cm/30in S:45cm/18in

The lovely pale blue scabious and its white forms are not easy to grow. In a light but fertile soil in full sun with adequate moisture they may flourish for many years, producing their graceful flowers on long slender stems throughout the summer. In less than ideal conditions, though, they are short-lived and require frequent division and careful nurture of the divided pieces until they are well rooted. However, scabious is a wonderful plant among pale yellow flowers, to lighten dark red and purple schemes or to hover over grey foliage.

SIDALCEA malviflora

H:90cm/36in   S:35cm/15in

Sidalceas resemble small, slender, single pink hollyhocks with a mound of finely cut foliage extending in summer into a tapering spire of pale or deep rose pink flowers, often delicately veined. They are especially attractive in a sea of catmint which emphasizes the pink of their sometimes purple-pink flowers but they will also provide a vertical accent among old roses, or among hummocks of dwarf purple berberis or rue.

SOLIDAGO hybrids

Goldenrod

H:30–150cm/12–60in   S:30–75cm/ 12–30in

Goldenrod used to signify a coarse, inva-sive plant with flowers of brassy yellow turning dingy brown almost as soon as they opened. The modern varieties of goldenrod, however, are clump-forming, clear or pale yellow and long lasting. 'Mimosa' is the tallest and earliest of several good varieties, flowering in mid-summer. 'Goldenmosa' is later and shor-ter. Shorter still and a very pale yellow is 'Lemore', while the season ends with the deep yellow *caesia*. If the same form and colour are required at the edge of the border, 'Golden Thumb' (syn. 'Queenie') and the slightly taller and earlier 'Crown of Rays' will provide weeks of colour through the autumn. All will live for several years without attention but are easily lifted and divided when they do become congested.

THALICTRUM delavayi

Meadow rue

H:1.2m/4ft   S:45cm/18in

This is one of the most graceful of all herbaceous perennials with foliage re-sembling a grey maidenhair fern and small lilac flowers in huge airy panicles. Even more enchanting is 'Hewitt's Double' in which each flower is a small rosette. The flower stems need individual staking.

Sadly, this lovely plant only succeeds in sheltered situations on moist, rich, leafy soil. In less ideal conditions, *T. aquilegi-folium* is a good substitute, with flowers forming compact, rounded heads of fluffy lilac. There is also a beautiful white form. Where even this will not grow, *T. spe-ciosissimum* (syn. *T. flavum glaucum*) will. It, too, has glaucous leaves, more robust

than the others, but the flower heads are taller and fluffy lemon yellow, thriving on dry soils and in some shade.

VERONICA species

H:1.5m/5ft   S:45cm/18in

V. virginica is a tall stately plant, standing perfectly erect with widely spaced leaves held horizontally, and tapering spikes of small flowers produced in late summer. In the species these are pale blue but the white form is more striking. It is good for the back of the border but even better in the middle ground where its silhouette can be appreciated.

There are many other attractive veronicas, from the spring flowering *V. gentianoides* with pale blue spires over flat dark green rosettes to *V. spicata* in which the colours of the spikes have been extended to include white and dusky red. *V. spicata incana,* with deep blue spikes over silvery grey mats of foliage, is an excellent edging plant.

VIOLA cornuta

H:25cm/10in   S:35cm/15in

This pert little viola produces quantities of flowers in early summer. On a moist rich soil it will luxuriate, climbing into shrubs and engulfing smaller herbaceous plants, but it is easily controlled by pulling off unwanted stems. If sheared after the main flush of flower it will regain something of its compactness and produce a second crop of flowers in late summer. The colour varies from deep lilac to pale silvery lilac and white. All give good ground cover beneath roses or hemerocallis, phlox and other clump-forming herbaceous plants.

Many of the old hybrid violas have been rescued from obscurity in recent years and these, too, are lovely plants with a wide colour range, but they need good soil and regular replacement by cuttings so are not suitable for the labour-saving garden.

LEFT *Veronica gentianoides*
RIGHT *Viola* hybrid

SUB-SHRUBS

These occupy a position in the plant world somewhere between tender perennials, herbaceous perennials and shrubs. They are hardier than tender perennials and will usually survive in sheltered situations for several years. In very mild areas they may eventually form quite large, woody shrubs. Top growth will be killed back in severe winters but the plants will shoot from ground level in the following spring like herbaceous perennials. They are seldom long-lived plants but are easily renewed by rooting cuttings.

CALCEOLARIA integrifolia

H:45cm/18in   S:45cm/18in
This bright lemon-yellow shrubby calceolaria with pale green, attractively wrinkled foliage is almost hardy in warm regions and is easily overwintered by rooting cuttings in cold climates. In the nineteenth century it was bedded in concentric rings with purple heliotrope and scarlet salvia and, not surprisingly, fell

from favour. However, it is a refreshing sight amongst golden feverfew, white petunias or antirrhinums and blue salvias.

CARYOPTERIS × clandonensis

H:75cm/30in   S:75cm/30in
Best on a well-drained soil in full sun, caryopteris has slender, arching branches clad in long, toothed grey-green leaves and bearing loose rounded heads of blue flowers in autumn. The conspicuous anthers of each flower contribute to the softness of the plant. In sheltered gardens or against a sunny wall it will grow larger than indicated but becomes bare and lanky, so it is better pruned hard in early spring. 'Arthur Simmonds' and the deeper 'Kew Blue' are among the best of the varieties.

CHEIRANTHUS and ERYSIMUM hybrids

Perennial wallflowers
H:15–45cm/6–18in   S:20–45cm/8–18in
The perennial wallflowers share their biennial brothers' sweet scent, but the flowers are smaller and carried on more compact

plants that, on poor, alkaline soils especially, will live for several years.

C. cheiri 'Harpur Crewe' is an upright, bright green bush with spikes of charming double, deep yellow and heavily scented flowers in spring. *E.* 'Moonlight' is low-growing, seldom more than 10cm/4in high, and a very pale yellow which glows in moonlight. 'Rufus' is a low bright orange while 'Bowles' Mauve' makes a large, spreading bush covered with mauve-grey flowers for much of the summer. *E. linifolium* 'Variegatum' has flowers of a similar colour on a brightly white-variegated plant and *E. mutabile* has long-lasting flower spikes in subtle shades of lavender-grey and brown, changing as they open.

EUPATORIUM ligustrinum

H:90cm/36in   S:60cm/24in
In sheltered gardens, this eupatorium will grow into a shrub 1.5m/5ft or more in height. It suffers die-back in severe winters and may even be killed to ground level. However, it is a more elegant plant after severe pruning and is best propagated each year or cut back to the ground like a herbaceous perennial to encourage young growth with dark glossy leaves and, in autumn, flat heads of fluffy white flowers.

FUCHSIA hybrids

H:60–120cm/24–48in   S:75–120cm/30–48in
Many fuchsias are distinctly tender but easily overwintered as rooted cuttings to plant outside in summer. Others are hardier and some will make large shrubs in sheltered areas, being cut back only in severe winters.

Among the less hardy types, 'Ting a Ling' (all white), 'Checkerboard' (slender, red and white), 'Marinka' (red and deep purple) and 'Chang' (an unusual soft orange) have small single flowers. 'Mrs Popple' (rounded red and purple flowers), 'Alice Hoffman' (red and white) and 'Tom Thumb' (a low red and purple) are reliably

Erysimum 'Bowles' Mauve'

hardy while 'Riccartonii', with small red and purple flowers and *Fuchsia magellanica molinae*, a pale green plant with pale pink flowers, form arching shrubs 1.8m/6ft or more tall. *F.m.* 'Versicolor', slightly less hardy, has smoky grey-pink foliage.

PEROVSKIA atriplicifolia

Russian sage
H:1.2m/4ft S:45cm/18in
Russian sage is a stiffly upright plant, the stems clad in slender, toothed leaves and terminated in autumn by narrow spikes of small deep violet flowers. The stems and leaves are silver-grey, a beautiful foil for the flowers, and this colour is retained on the leafless stems through the winter. Even if the plant escapes winter damage, it is wise to prune it almost to ground level in spring to encourage young shoots.

In large drifts it forms a perfect setting for pale pink sedums, pink and mauve asters and white, pink or lavender colchicums and true autumn crocus.

PHYGELIUS aequalis, P. capensis

H:60–120cm/24–48in S:75cm/30in
Phygelius aequalis, a low, wide-spreading plant with numerous spikes of salmon pink tubular flowers in summer and often into autumn, should be cut to the ground in winter. A clear, pale yellow form is rapidly gaining in popularity for use in large pots or in well-drained borders. *P. capensis* is hardier and more erect, often retaining a woody base and producing loose panicles of deep orange flowers. Trained on a wall it will reach 2–3m/7–10ft tall with its flowers held well clear of the foliage. Hybrids between the two species are beginning to appear with flowers of peach or dusky red.

ROMNEYA × hybrida

Tree poppy
H:1.5m/5ft S:1.8m/6ft
In a mild climate, romneya will grow into a very large shrub but, in cooler climates, it will be cut close to the ground by frost

Fuchsia triphylla 'Gartenmeister Bonnstadt'

to emerge in spring with vigorous stems clad in deeply toothed, glaucous grey leaves. Huge white poppies with round masses of yellow stamens are produced in late summer and autumn. Difficult to establish (being best planted carefully from pots in spring), it will only flourish on well-drained soils, but once established it will spread rapidly underground and can become a beautiful nuisance. Planted against a wall with the stiffer *Fremontodendron californicum* to echo the yellow centre of the flowers and pale clematis to harmonize with the glaucous leaf and white flower, it will remain beautiful for many months.

SALVIA officinalis

Sage
H:45cm/18in S:45cm/18in
The culinary sage is useful for its soft, aromatic foliage and for the spikes of purple flowers in late summer. It is not long-lived, even on the poor, dry soils in

which it flourishes, so it should be pruned hard in spring to rejuvenate it and replaced frequently with young plants that are easily grown from cuttings.

The common sage has leaves of a subdued grey-green, a delightful foil for flowers of any colour and a useful intermediary between silver-grey and more bright green foliage. Purple sage (*S.o.* 'Purpurascens') has foliage of a soft plum-purple, wonderful in grey or bronze schemes and with red and purple flowers. *S.o.* 'Icterina' has leaves variegated brightly with yellow and is equally useful in winter, as a foil to aconites and early daffodils, and in summer when it provides a setting for calceolarias and yellow antirrhinums. *S.o.* 'Tricolor' has purple leaves splashed with cream and pink. Sadly it is not a vigorous variety but, if replaced from cuttings each year, it is excellent as a young plant with *Berberis thunbergii* 'Rose Glow', rue and other grey foliage.

ROSES

The rose is more versatile today than ever before in its history, ranging from miniature patio roses to climbers which will scale large trees, from low ground-cover roses to large shrubs. In between are the undeniably beautiful, colourful, prolific and often fragrant bush roses.

Many people consider that the rose should be grown in isolation in special rose gardens, although even they must admit that the appearance will be enhanced with an edging of some kind, some London pride, perhaps, or pinks or violas. It is not a big step to vary the underplanting and finally to incorporate the roses into a mixed border where their flowers can be enjoyed and their often ungainly stems concealed. With once-flowering shrub roses it makes even more sense to immerse the plants in a tapestry of other flowers, using the often attractive foliage of the roses as a background to herbaceous plants and summer bulbs.

SPECIES ROSES

The species roses, with their charming single flowers, are little known in gardens. Among them, though, are many lovely plants.

Rosa chinensis 'Mutabilis' (H:1.5m/5ft S:1.5m/5ft), a single China rose, bears a constant succession of fragrant flowers opening from orange buds, fading to buff and deepening to coppery pink as they age. It is a frail rose, damaged by cold weather, but on a warm wall will continue to grow and flower with great freedom, reaching 6m/20ft or more.

Rosa fedtschenkoana (H:2.5m/8ft S:3m/10ft) is a vigorous suckering shrub and fiercely prickly. However, its arching branches, clothed in pale grey foliage and bearing large, single white flowers all along the branch from midsummer make

Rosa gallica 'Versicolor'

it wonderful for the larger grey garden.

Rosa glauca (H:2m/7ft S:2m/7ft), better known as *R. rubrifolia*, with small, pale pink flowers, is grown for its pale, grey-blue foliage on arching maroon stems. It is lovely with grey or purple foliage and with red-purple and white flowers. It can be grown into a large shrub or pruned to fit into the smallest garden.

Rosa hugonis (H:2m/7ft S:2m/7ft) is a model of grace and charm with very fine textured foliage on dark maroon branches, wreathed in early summer with cascades of small, pale yellow, cup-shaped flowers followed by dark red-brown hips. The plant forms an attractive mound, lovely in winter for its stem colour as well as during the summer.

Rosa moyesii 'Geranium' (H:3m/10ft S:2.5m/8ft) is stiffly upright with small leaves and brilliant scarlet-red flowers. Its main attraction, though, is the display of long glowing scarlet hips that follow the flowers and last into winter. Although large, its upright growth makes it suitable for small gardens where it can arch over-head.

OLD SHRUB ROSES

In recent decades there has been a resurgence of interest in the old shrub roses with their petal-packed flowers, wonderful fragrance and strong, disease-free growth.

'Alba Maxima' (H:2m/7ft S:2m/7ft) is a vigorous and trouble-free shrub with huge clusters of very fragrant, flat, charmingly quartered flowers in midsummer. The flowers are white and, as with other Alba roses, the leaves are large and pale green.

'Cécile Brunner' (H:1m/3ft), 'Bloomfield Abundance' (H:2m/7ft) and 'Climbing Cécile Brunner' (H:6m/20ft) are a trio of charming roses with nearly identical flowers on plants of very different size. The flowers are tiny, exquisitely formed and sweetly fragrant, unfurling pale pink from high pointed buds and borne on slender stems throughout the summer.

'Charles de Mills' (H:1.5m/5ft S:2m/

Rosa rugosa 'Frau Dagmar Hastrup'

7ft) is a Gallica rose with enormous quantities of very flat, deep crimson and heavily fragrant flowers borne along its strong, arching branches in midsummer. The flowers fade to magenta-purple as they age and are lovely with foxgloves and geraniums.

R. gallica 'Versicolor' (H:1m/3ft S:1m/3ft) could equally well be listed with the species roses but its very double flowers of pale pink splashed irregularly with deep red seem more appropriate with the old hybrids. It has been known in gardens as 'Rosa Mundi', for at least three centuries and is a vigorous, low, prickly shrub, flowering with enormous freedom in midsummer. It is equally suitable for the flower border or as a low hedge.

RUGOSA ROSES

H:2m/7ft   S:2m/7ft

This attractive and useful species has bright green, deeply wrinkled and disease-free foliage and a succession of large, single, strong magenta and very fragrant flowers on a suckering and fiercely prickly shrub. The flowers are followed by large scarlet hips, which are rich in vitamin C, and the leaves turn a clear yellow before falling in the autumn. It grows particularly well on acid sandy soils but is amenable to heavier and alkaline soils or even chalk if well-cultivated. It has given rise to a number of even more beautiful varieties, many of which flower over the whole summer.

'Agnes' is unusual in having large, double flowers of soft yellow, a characteristic inherited from its other parent, *R. foetida*.

'Blanc Double de Coubert' has double flowers of a papery pure white, unfortunately turning brown as they age, but it is a very beautiful rose.

'Frau Dagmar Hastrup' grows only 1m/3ft high with clusters of single, pure pale pink flowers that clash in midseason with the scarlet hips, a fault that can be forgiven.

Rosa 'Penelope'

Rosa 'Constance Spry'

'Hunter' is a rugosa/hybrid tea cross with flowers of a deep, rich red but with the vigour, fragrance and foliage of *R. rugosa*.

'Roseraie de l'Hay' is perhaps the best of the rugosas, with double flowers of vivid magenta-crimson freely produced through summer and autumn.

Rugosa 'Alba' has pure white, single flowers opening from faintly pink-tinted buds, followed by large hips.

'Sarah van Fleet' is taller than most, reaching 3m/10ft if allowed, with silvery pink, single flowers over a long season. Unlike the other rugosas it is stiffly upright and quickly becomes bare at the base but this can easily be disguised by planting below it.

MODERN SHRUB ROSES

The modern shrub roses are a diverse group that have in common beautiful flowers produced freely throughout the season on an attractive shrub.

'Buff Beauty', with huge trusses of pale buff-yellow flowers over bronze foliage, and 'Penelope', with more open clusters of very pale pink, are hybrid musk roses, forerunners of the modern shrubs. Both make large plants, 2m/7ft high and wide and laden with fragrant flowers in mid-summer, but they can easily be reduced in size by pruning if necessary.

'Chianti' (deep crimson-purple), 'Constance Spry' (clear pink), 'Charles Austin' (apricot) and 'Graham Stuart Thomas' (butter-yellow) are English roses, produced by David Austin to combine the quartered flower of old roses with modern rose colours and repeat flowering. The first two, which make very large shrubs, flower once only but are magnificent in flower; the others are lower-growing, 1m/3ft high and wide, and perpetual flowering with the delightful form and fragrance of the old roses.

'Altissimo' (bright crimson), 'Golden Wings' (pale yellow on lovely grey-green foliage), 'Nevada' (cream-white) and 'White Wings' (white with red stamens) are large-flowered (very large in the case of 'Altissimo') single roses of great charm on arching, upright shrubs. 'White Wings' is less vigorous than the others but worth persevering with.

'Lavender Lassie' and 'Magenta' are medium-sized shrubs (1.5m/5ft high and wide) with large clusters of flowers in intriguing shades of lavender, pink, grey and magenta, loved by flower arrangers and delightful with buff-yellow and mauve flowers such as the perennial wall-flowers, penstemons and some phlox.

CLIMBING ROSES

There are three main groups of climbing roses.

The climbing sports of hybrid tea and floribunda roses are essentially very long, thin rose bushes that tend to flower only at the top unless carefully pruned. Many are fragrant and most will produce a second crop of flowers after the main midsummer

RIGHT *Rosa* 'Sympathie'

Rosa 'Swan Lake'

flush. Among the best are 'Paul's Lemon Pillar' (lemon fading to white), 'Gloire de Dijon' (buff-yellow, very hardy and continuous), 'Zéphirine Drouhin' (deep pink, heavily fragrant and perpetual flowering on thornless stems) and 'Climbing Etoile de Hollande' (fragrant deep crimson).

The second group are the pillar roses or modern climbers. These have been bred for a more compact habit and for freedom of flowering throughout the season. They are essentially large shrubs (ideal for the back of a border) that can be tied up to pillars and other supports and trained along pergolas but not for any great distance. Included in this group are 'Swan Lake' (white), 'New Dawn' (a very old silvery pink), 'Sympathie' (dark crimson), 'Golden Showers' (exceptionally free-

flowering and good on a shaded wall) and 'Schoolgirl' (apricot-orange).

The rambler roses are very vigorous, often growing 10m/30ft or more with huge clusters of rather small flowers in midsummer and little if any repeat flowering. They can be trained over large pergolas, along walls and fences or up into large trees. If kept within bounds by pruning, they create a wonderful abundance of flower even in a small garden and their lack of flowers later in the season can be compensated for by training late-flowering clematis through them. Among the ramblers are 'Wedding Day' (huge trusses of buff yellow fading to white), 'Easlea's Golden Rambler' (butter yellow), 'Adelaide d'Orléans' (pale pink in pendulous sprays), 'Paul's Scarlet Climber' (bril-

liant scarlet) and 'Veilchenblau' (an intriguing rose with magenta buds fading to lilac-grey).

HYBRID TEA AND FLORIBUNDA ROSES

The hybrid tea roses were developed essentially for exhibition and as cut flowers with one large, beautifully scrolled bud on each stem unfurling into a large flower of crimson, clear pink, white or golden yellow, but with a small number of smaller buds below. The crossing of hybrid teas with dwarf polyantha roses, which have huge clusters of small, mop-like flowers on each stem, resulted in the floribundas that have fewer flowers in each cluster. The fusion is now so complete that it is difficult to differentiate between hybrid teas and floribundas, and the more recent classification into large-flowered and bunch-flowered roses does nothing to ease this difficulty. Both hybrid teas and floribundas combine a wide range of colour (increased in recent decades to include coppery orange), freedom of flowering, some fragrance and healthy, glossy, disease-resistant foliage.

Particularly attractive hybrid teas include: 'Alec's Red' (deep crimson), 'Blessings' (pale salmon pink), 'Tynwald' (ivory white), 'Elizabeth Harkness' (very pale buff), 'Whisky Mac' (copper-orange and very fragrant) and 'King's Ransom' (deep yellow).

Among the floribundas the following offer a wide colour range: 'Europeana' (very dark crimson on bronze foliage), 'Dearest' (salmon pink), 'English Miss' (very pale pink), 'Iceberg' (white, ageing to pink, very vigorous), 'Chanelle' (pale buff-pink), 'Apricot Nectar' (delightful pale copper-pink), 'Glenfiddich' (deep copper-orange and very fragrant), 'Korresia' (bright, pure yellow), 'Lavender Pinocchio' (magenta-grey) and 'Café' (a fascinating blend of peach-brown).

FLOWERING SHRUBS

The main purpose of shrubs in the garden is to provide structure, but I have focused here on those shrubs whose abundant, beautiful and perhaps fragrant flowers make them as suitable for the flower garden as for the larger landscape of the shrub garden. Most of these also have attractive foliage and many provide support for the more slender climbers.

ABELIA × grandiflora

H:1.2m/4ft   S:1.2m/4ft

This is a graceful, small, dense shrub, semi-evergreen with pointed leaves of a glossy dark green becoming bronze in autumn and winter. From late summer until autumn frosts it carries numerous clusters of soft pink tubular flowers each held in a deeper maroon-pink calyx that remains after the flower has fallen. It needs full sun and a well-drained soil, and may be damaged in severe winters.

Abelia looks lovely with bronze-purple foliage, with pale pink roses, purple fuchsias and blue *Gentiana asclepiadea* or agapanthus.

ABUTILON vitifolium

H:2.5m/8ft   S:2m/7ft

A tall, upright shrub with densely hairy grey-green leaves, *A. vitifolium* produces quantities of large, pale lavender flowers throughout the summer. The depth of colouring varies and there is a beautiful white form. Although thriving only in sheltered, well-drained situations, it grows quickly and is easily replaced if killed in a severe winter. Self-sown seedlings often arise around the original plant.

Wonderful with grey foliage, pink, lavender and white flowers, it also complements yellow and buff flowers, from the delicate apricot of modern floribunda roses to clear yellow *Hypericum* 'Hidcote'.

Abutilon vitifolium album

AMELANCHIER lamarckii

Snowy mespilus, shad bush
H:3m/10ft   S:1.5m/5ft

Although ultimately a small tree, this amelanchier will take some years to reach its maximum height and may be kept smaller indefinitely by pruning. There is some confusion over the name and there are various plants available under the names of *A. canadensis*, × *grandiflora, laevis* and *lamarckii*. It is safest to buy container-grown amelanchier in flower in spring and to pick out the plants with translucent bronze young foliage and long, loose racemes of soft white flowers.

Its beauty lies not only in its young foliage and delicate clouds of flower but also in its elegant summer foliage and brilliant red autumn colour. It is particularly lovely with pheasant's eye narcissus, forget-me-nots and other delicate spring flowers and makes a good background plant during summer. It is very hardy, best in moist, peaty soils but tolerates alkaline soils if they are not too dry.

BUDDLEJA species

Butterfly bush
H:2m/7ft   S:1.5m/5ft

Best known of the buddlejas is *B. davidii*, with long spikes of purple, lilac, pink, red or white flowers in late summer and autumn, adored by butterflies. *B. fallowiana* is rather smaller and more elegant with grey foliage and pale lilac spikes. Much less well-known is the delightful *B. × weyeriana*, with tapering clusters of pink-tinged buds opening to deep buff flowers with a bright orange eye. All these flower on new growth and should be pruned almost to the ground each spring.

Buddleja alternifolia is more like a small, grey weeping willow and can be trained as a standard to make a beautiful substitute for willow in small gardens. Left to itself it quickly grows into a large mound of silvery foliage 6m/20ft or more across with small clusters of lavender flowers all along the branches in summer. However, it is best pruned after flowering.

CEANOTHUS species and hybrids

Californian lilac
H:1–3m/3–10ft   S:1–3m/3–10ft
C. impressus derives its name from the deeply impressed veins of its small, dark evergreen leaves but it could equally apply to the impressive display of deep blue flowers that cover the plant in late spring. Being unreliably hardy it is usually grown as a wall plant, but it can be grown as a very large free-standing mound. If killed in a severe winter it is easily and quickly replaced.

C. 'Autumnal Blue', also best against a wall, creates a similar effect with somewhat looser flower clusters in late summer and autumn.

C. × *delinianus* includes a number of delightful sub-shrubs with soft, feathery panicles of flower. Among the best are 'Marie Simon' with pale pink flowers in early summer and red stems in winter, 'Indigo', a rich purple-blue, and 'Gloire de Versailles', a taller growing plant with powder-blue flowers in summer and autumn.

CHAENOMELES × superba

Japonica, quince
H:1m/3ft   S:2m/7ft
Flowering quince has glossy dark green leaves in summer and ropes of colourful flowers along its bare stems at the end of winter. The brightest is 'Knap Hill Scarlet'. There are many other varieties with flowers of crimson, pink, blush or white. They will grow in sun or shade and may be trained flat against a wall, as a fan, cordon or espalier, or allowed to sprawl forward as a low, free-growing shrub.

Chaenomeles × superba

CHOISYA ternata

Mexican orange
H:1.2m/4ft   S:2m/7ft
This attractive shrub has a wide mound of glossy, pale evergreen foliage with clusters of sweet-smelling white blossom in late spring/early summer and often again in autumn. Because it is not especially hardy and may be disfigured by snow or freezing winds it is thought of as a shrub for sunny walls only, but it will thrive against a shaded wall where it is protected from frosts and sudden thaws. The foliage is unpleasantly aromatic so avoid planting choisya where it will be brushed against. 'Sundance' is a new variety with bright golden yellow foliage.

CISTUS × corbariensis

Sun rose
H:50cm/20in   S:1.2m/4ft
There are many cistus ranging from large shrubs to low ground covers. *C.* × *corbariensis* is one of the hardiest and most useful, making a widespreading compact mound of sage-green foliage that turns deep purple in the winter. In summer it is covered in 2.5cm/1in diameter flowers with crumpled white petals emerging from crimson buds. Although each flower lasts only for one day this is a delightful plant that grows well in dry soils and spills out informally from the border, blending well with lavenders, grey-leaved plants and soft-coloured roses or forming an excellent setting for potentillas, hypericums and other bright colours.

CORONILLA glauca

H:75cm/30in   S:75cm/30in
Given well-drained soil and a sunny position, this provides a low mound of glaucous grey foliage all year round and small, sweetly scented deep yellow flowers in abundance in late spring and often in autumn. Coronilla is not a long-lived plant. It may be pruned if it becomes straggly, or can be easily replaced from seed. It is lovely with *Clematis macropetala*.

CYTISUS battandieri

Pineapple broom
H:2.5m/8ft   S:2m/7ft
This tall, elegant shrub is covered in silky silver leaves from spring to autumn and, in midsummer, each lateral branch produces a pineapple-shaped and pineapple-scented cluster of rich yellow flowers. It is often grown as a wall shrub, benefitting from the shelter of a sunny wall, but will also make an attractively arching free-standing large shrub. The temptation to tidy up wall-grown plants in spring should be avoided as this will remove much of the flowering wood. Instead, shorten the shoots to a few buds after flowering.

DAPHNE species

H:60–90cm/24–36in   S:90cm/36in
Daphne × *burkwoodii* is an upright semi-evergreen mound of small, grey-green leaves, covered in early summer with fragrant pale-pink flowers. It often flowers again less freely in late summer or early autumn. It is quick-growing, and will

Choisya ternata

often exceed the height indicated.

D. mezereum carries tight wands of purple-pink flowers on stiffly upright leafless branches in late winter and early spring, followed by scarlet berries among its young, grey-green leaves. Its white variety has yellow berries. Both are fragrant in flower, wonderful plants to have near the house to enjoy with dusky hellebores and the earliest crocus.

D. odora 'Aureo-marginata' is a lower evergreen mound with beautiful glossy yellow-green leaves broadly margined with cream and small, intensely fragrant purple flowers in late winter and early spring. Surprisingly, this variegated form is hardier than the species itself.

Hamamelis mollis

HAMAMELIS mollis

Witch hazel
H:2m/7ft   S:2m/7ft
The slow-growing Chinese witch hazel will eventually exceed the dimensions indicated but the lower branches can be removed to turn it into a wide-spreading small tree.

It is one of the most beautiful of the winter-flowering plants, with dark branches carrying clusters of fragrant spidery-petalled yellow flowers for two months or more in late winter. It is lovely underplanted with snowdrops and winter aconites. The woolly leaf-buds expand into grey-green leaves that eventually turn clear yellow in autumn.

HEBE hulkeana

H:75cm/30in   S:1m/3ft
The flowers of hebe are often of secondary interest to their evergreen foliage, but *H. hulkeana* is also an outstanding flowering shrub. It has uncharacteristically informal growth: long, slender branches with widely spaced glossy green leaves edged thinly with maroon. In early summer each branch ends with a long, spreading panicle of small, pale lavender flowers so the whole plant is covered in a foam of blossom. It may be allowed to sprawl gracefully over the edge of a border or it can be trained on a wall, where it may reach 1.8m/6ft or more in mild areas.

HIBISCUS syriacus

H:2m/7ft   S:1.5m/5ft
This upright, sparsely branched plant has attractive grey-green foliage. Although perfectly hardy, it will only produce its autumn flowers freely after a hot summer and the flower buds will only open on sunny days. In temperate climates it needs a sheltered position.

Given favourable conditions, it will produce exotic single or double flowers in red, pink, purple, blue or white through the autumn months, contrasting in form with the more common buddlejas, caryopteris and other autumn shrubs and harmonizing beautifully in colour. It thrives in a rich soil and responds well to severe pruning if it becomes too large.

HYDRANGEA paniculata,
H. serrata 'Preziosa'

H:2m/7ft   S:1.5m/5ft
The dozens of lacecap and mop-head hydrangeas with rounded flower heads of pink, purple, blue or white on mounds of yellow-green leaves are too well known to need description, useful though they are in the flower garden. *H. paniculata* is a more upright plant with tapering pyramids of white flowers tinged pink with age, produced on the current year's growth in late summer or autumn. It should be pruned

almost to the ground in spring, before the leaves appear and, given the moist, fertile soil on which all hydrangeas thrive, it will produce shoots 2m/7ft or more long crowned with long panicles of flower. In *H.p.* 'Grandiflora', the huge panicles are composed entirely of large sterile florets and the effect of the solid pyramids of flower hovers between spectacular and gross. *H.p.* 'Tardiva', however, has sterile florets irregularly interspersed among small fertile florets and the effect is undeniably beautiful.

H. serrata 'Preziosa' (H:90cm/36in S:75cm/30in) is a small upright form of mop-head hydrangea. The leaves are purple-tinged when young and the flowers deepen from pink to reddish-purple as autumn advances. It is a charming, small hydrangea and ideal for imparting a deeper colour to the misty lavenders of buddlejas and other autumn flowers.

HYPERICUM 'Hidcote'

H:1.2m/4ft   S:1.2m/4ft

One of the longest-flowering of all shrubs, it produces its globular rich yellow flowers freely from midsummer into late autumn on mounds of grey-green, semi-evergreen foliage. Although the inner colour of the flower is bright, the whole aspect of the plant is charming and informal, more like a herbaceous plant than a shrub, except in winter when the red-brown colour of the stems creates a welcome warm glow.

JASMINUM humile 'Revolutum'

H:2m/7ft   S:2m/7ft

The elegantly toothed dark green leaves and clusters of slender fragrant flowers borne freely all along the stem in early summer resemble summer jasmine, but the bright yellow flowers and the stout bright green stems are more like the winter-flowering species.

It forms a handsome arching shrub, nearly evergreen in mild winters and is a great asset in the border throughout the year.

Hydrangea paniculata 'Tardiva'

Hypericum 'Hidcote'

Kerria japonica

KERRIA japonica

H:1m/3ft   S:1.5m/5ft

This is best known for its double form *K.j.* 'Pleniflora', a stiffly upright suckering shrub, often exceeding 3m/10ft in height against a wall, with double flowers of ragged, orange-yellow petals. It is a striking and adaptable plant if rather coarse. The species itself is a slender, spreading shrub with zig-zag stems of bright green that are attractive in winter and buttercup-yellow flowers like small single roses in spring. The foliage is long, slender and fresh pale green. Even more graceful is *K.j.* 'Picta', with sparkling white-variegated foliage that emerges after the flowers. All three grow in sun or shade.

MAHONIA japonica

H:1.2m/4ft   S:1.5m/5ft

Although the named forms of *M.* × *media* have more conspicuous flowers than their hardier parent, *M. japonica* combines handsome, broad, soft-green foliage and long racemes of fragrant pale yellow flowers from late autumn to early spring with a more relaxed habit of growth. Side shoots grow out to form a wide mound resting on the ground, eventually much larger than indicated above.

In addition to its winter beauty, it provides a bold foliage group during the summer and many of the older leaves turn a rich red in autumn. It will grow well in shade or sun.

PHILADELPHUS species and hybrids

Mock orange

H:1–3m/3–10ft   S:1.5–2m/5–7ft

All the philadelphus have white flowers in midsummer. Sometimes the flowers are double, sometimes stained purple at the base of the petal and usually deliciously fragrant. The main variation is in the size of the plant. Old, unpruned plants of *P. coronarius* may grow to 6m/20ft; *P. microphyllus*, the larger-leaved, larger-flowered 'Boule d'Argent' and 'Manteau d'Hermine' seldom exceed 1m/3ft. *P. microphyllus* is scarcely recognizable as a mock orange with its frail arching stems, tiny dark green leaves and dense form, until it produces its myriads of small, powerfully fragrant flowers. It is a lovely shrub for the small garden. 'Sybille' (1.2m/4ft) and 'Belle Etoile' (1.8m/6ft) are more typical and strongly scented, while *P. coronarius* 'Aureus' has bright golden-yellow leaves to set off its fragrant white flowers, especially if hard-pruned after flowering.

POTENTILLA fruticosa and varieties

H:45–75cm/18–30in   S:60–120cm/24–48in

The shrubby potentillas are neat, low-growing mounds with small, soft green or grey leaves on densely branched twigs.

The flowers, borne over a very long season in summer and autumn, are usually yellow or white, although delicate shades of peach-orange have been available for many years, 'Red Ace', with bright scarlet flowers, is more recent and 'Princess', a charming pale, clear pink, is newer still. Most are extremely hardy and will grow in dry soil or by water, but the orange-stained varieties are best grown in partial shade as the colours fade in bright sunlight. Other varieties include *mandschurica*, low growing with grey leaves and white flowers; 'Vilmoriniana', upright with very silky leaves and creamy white flowers; 'Primrose Beauty' and 'Maanelys' ('Moonlight'), pale yellow; 'Elizabeth', with large flowers of butter yellow; and 'Tangerine', orange-red fading to yellow in sun.

SPIRAEA nipponica 'Snowmound'

H:1.2m/4ft   S:1.2m/4ft

Among the most beautiful of its genus, 'Snowmound' has gracefully arching stems, attractively red-brown in winter, bowed down in early summer by rounded clusters of white flowers forming a cascade of white blossom. As the flowers fade the new leaves expand to their full size; they are a pleasant glaucous green that is a lovely foil for many other flowers. The old wood should be removed after flowering. Although it will grow to 1.2m/4ft quite quickly, it is a useful plant towards

Viburnum plicatum 'Mariesii'

the front of the border for the sake of its fountainlike silhouette of neatly toothed grey-green foliage.

SYRINGA vulgaris

Lilac

H:3m/10ft   S:2m/7ft

Lilac begins life as an upright shrub and may be kept this way by careful pruning. Alternatively it can be left to grow with the lower branches removed to form a picturesque small tree, allowing other plants to grow underneath. The long spikes of delicately scented flowers, ranging from white to deep purple (yellow in the variety 'Primrose'), and from airy single to crowded double are a sure sign that spring is giving way to summer. They associate beautifully with old double peonies of deep red, silvery pink or white, and with tulips of almost any colour.

In gardens that are too small for the common lilac, *S. × persica*, the fern-leaved *S. laciniata* and the diminutive *S. meyeri* 'Palibin' provide charming smaller alternatives.

VIBURNUM species

H:1.5–3m/5–10ft   S:1.5–3m/5–10ft

Among more than a hundred species of viburnum there are five of particular value. *V. × bodnantense* flowers throughout the winter with fragrant pink flowers on a tall, upright shrub. In summer it has burnished leaves, and the twiggy stems provide a good support for clematis. *V. tinus* is also winter-flowering, with flat heads of faintly pink-tinged flowers, but its evergreen dark rounded mass forms a good summer backdrop. *V. carlesii* is spring-flowering, with rounded clusters of blush white, intensely fragrant flowers just ahead of its pale grey-green leaves. *V. plicatum* 'Mariesii' has a spectacular array of white flowers ranged along horizontal tiers of pale green foliage in early summer. It requires moist soil and plenty of space. *V. opulus*, has flat heads of white flowers in early summer and there is a sterile form, aptly named the snowball bush. The many forms of *V. opulus* all share the bright green foliage of the species and its rich autumn colour.

CLIMBERS

The main purpose of climbers is to soften the hard lines of walls and fences, but many have beautiful flowers as well. All require some support. Some are self-clinging on rough surfaces, others need wires or slender trellis for their twining stems or tendrils and the least vigorous may be allowed to scramble through a shrub or robust herbaceous perennial.

As the size of climbers depends on the training they receive rather than on the species itself, no dimensions are given. Instead they have been classified as slow or fast climbers.

CLEMATIS species and hybrids

Fast climbing

The most vigorous species clematis are best confined to walls and trellis unless they can be allowed to engulf old apple trees or climb into large trees (needing help to scale the trunk), but the finer species and the hybrids may also be allowed to climb through and over shrubs and even vigorous herbaceous perennials to harmonize in flower or to provide flowers later in the season.

C. cirrhosa balearica is the first to flower, producing small, pendant white flowers, heavily spotted with maroon in the best forms, during the winter months above finely dissected deep green foliage. *C. montana* and *C. macropetala* follow in late spring. The former, one of the most vigorous climbers, will climb through large trees or quickly clothe a trellis but it can be kept in bounds by pruning after flowering. It is white and fragrant, with pink, non-scented varieties. *C. macropetala* is more refined, with double, pale blue flowers and cream centres followed by delightful silky seed heads. Both will grow well on walls of any aspect. The large-flowered hybrids take over during

Clematis 'Madame le Coultre'

the summer but the vigorous *C. tangutica* with charming yellow lanterns starts in early autumn, followed by *C. viticella*, one of the daintiest species with fragile-looking purple flowers on long stems.

The large-flowered clematis hybrids fall into two groups. The first flower in late spring and early summer on old stems. Ideally, these varieties should be carefully pruned in early spring, removing any dead and weak stems and tying in the remaining strong growths. The reward will be a crop of large, double flowers on the old wood of many varieties followed by a succession of single flowers on new growth. Among these are 'Madame le Coultre' (white), 'Belle of Woking' (double silvery mauve), 'Vyvyan Pennell' (double lilac), 'Lasurstern' (blue), 'The President' (purple, with a very long flowering season) and 'Jackmanii Rubra' (double crimson).

The second group flower in late summer and autumn on young growth. These can be cut back in early spring to a strong pair of buds at the base of each stem, removing the whole of the top growth. The new shoots will quickly scramble up through trellis, shrubs or other support. These varieties include 'Huldine' (translucent white with mauve reverse), 'Perle d'Azur' (azure blue), 'Gipsy Queen' (violet purple), 'Niobe' (rich velvety red) and of course × *jackmanii*, a deep purple and the most popular clematis ever raised.

HYDRANGEA petiolaris

Slow climbing
Although it may need some support initially, the climbing hydrangea will soon cling to brickwork or rough stone with aerial rootlets. On smooth walls it can be woven through wire mesh or tied to wires or trellis. It is a handsome climber with red-brown peeling bark and the attractive remains of old flower heads in winter, polished pale green leaves in summer turning yellow in autumn, and large heads of white lace-cap flowers in midsummer borne on lateral branches standing well

Lonicera tragophylla

clear of the wall. It does especially well on a shady wall where the white flowers show to particular advantage.

JASMINUM nudiflorum, J. officinale

Fast climbing
J. nudiflorum (winter jasmine) is a versatile and cheering plant. A lank shrub rather than a true climber, it can be left to form a large, arching mound (in which case it will often root at the tips and spread into an extensive thicket), pruned hard each spring to form a more restrained fountain of growth, or tied up to a fence or wall, where it will easily reach a height of 6m/20ft. When a permanent framework has been established over the allocated wall space, lateral branches are simply cut back to the lowest pair of buds after flowering to provide a fresh crop of bright green stems for the following year. It flowers through the dreariest depths of winter, producing long wands of bright yellow flowers, and will succeed in shade as well as sun.

J. officinale (white or summer jasmine) is a twining plant that needs a trellis or wires for support. Its elegant dark green leaves are retained long into the autumn, falling to reveal a mass of tangled dull green stems. Grown against a warm wall it produces clusters of powerfully fragrant white flowers, luminous at dusk, from midsummer into autumn. In good condi-

Solanum crispum

Wisteria sinensis

tions it rapidly reaches 6–9m/20–30ft, scrambling up fences, over pergola beams and across wires to make a fragrant, sheltered bower.

LONICERA periclymenum

Honeysuckle, woodbine
Fast climbing
Grown as much for its sweet scent as for its colour, honeysuckle is a vigorous twining plant producing clusters of long tubular flowers, cream within and purple-flushed on the outside, in summer and intermittently into autumn. In warm summers it will set heavy crops of orange-red berries that remain into the winter. It can be pruned after flowering each year or left to grow into a large mass and then severely pruned at irregular intervals. Late Dutch honeysuckle, *L.p.* 'Serotina', has flowers of a deeper reddish-purple on the outside and will flower more freely into autumn.

There are many other beautiful honeysuckles, such as the clear yellow *L. tragophylla* and lovely orange *L. × tellmanniana*, both of which flourish in shade, but none combine the freedom of growth and flowering and the delicious fragrance of *L. periclymenum*.

SOLANUM crispum

Slow climbing
This is, in effect, a climbing potato, a semi-evergreen, scrambling shrub covered in late summer and autumn with yellow-centred purple flowers in large clusters. The colour will pick up the purple-blue of caryopteris, buddleja, perovskia and Michaelmas daisies, for which the solanum provides a useful backing especially on well-drained and chalky soils.

S. jasminoides is a true twining climber that will quickly reach 6–9m/20–30ft. Its white-flowered form is especially lovely, but it needs a very sheltered situation.

WISTERIA sinensis

Chinese wisteria
Fast climbing
Chinese wisteria will climb to the top of the tallest tree once it has reached into the lower branches for support, but it can also be restrained to fit into the smallest garden, surviving in a large pot for many years. Against a warm wall it will flower more freely and at an earlier age, producing its scented pale lilac flowers in early summer. The grey-green leaves are also quietly beautiful as are the spiralling stems. The secret of success with wisteria is not to let it grow too quickly and to train the main branches horizontally. Leading shoots should be cut back each year to encourage lateral branching and laterals should be pinched out after four to six leaves, then cut back to a few buds in winter. The result will be a sculptural plant draped in flowers rather than a thin tangle of naked stems flowering in the sky.

ANNUAL CLIMBERS

The ability of annual climbers to clothe their supports in a single season, to provide colour, fragrance and privacy, is of enormous value in an age when people move so often into new houses with new and featureless gardens. They are also attractive as tall pot plants and for trailing down from window boxes. All benefit from rich soil to encourage rapid growth.

CONVOLVULUS althaeoides

Seldom exceeding 1m/3ft high, this elegant plant has deeply cut silvery leaves and deep pink funnel flowers from late summer. It spreads underground but can be pulled up where it is unwelcome.

To show the foliage clearly it can be allowed to climb through a dark-leaved low shrub but it is more beautiful climbing through lavender hedges. Rosemary is also a good and slightly darker host.

In a well-drained, sheltered garden it may prove to be hardy. It can be propagated from root cuttings and planted out in spring.

ECCREMOCARPUS scaber

Easily grown as a half-hardy annual, eccremocarpus may survive mild winters, producing new growth from near ground level to flower earlier in the year than seed-raised plants. It climbs by tendrils to a height of 3–4m/10–15ft in a good summer and produces loose spikes of tubular flowers in crimson, brick red or warm yellow from late summer until frost, over dark green, neatly toothed

leaves. The slender growths can be allowed to climb up through earlier-flowering wall plants such as quince, winter jasmine and *Cytisus battandieri*, and will also adorn foliage climbers such as ivy and purple grape.

LATHYRUS odoratus

Sweet pea

Usually grown from seed sown individually or in small clusters in deep pots in early spring and planted out with a minimum of root disturbance, sweet peas may also be sown in late spring where they are to flower. They climb by tendrils on bean netting, up bamboo canes, or on pyramids of twiggy brushwood to make a vertical accent.

The charm of the sweet pea is its delicate perfume and wide range of soft and sometimes bright colours – white, cream,

Lathyrus odoratus

pink, lavender, purple, red, maroon or scarlet. Flowering is enhanced by a cool summer and regular removal of spent flowers.

PHASEOLUS vulgaris

Runner bean
The runner bean was introduced into cultivation as a flowering climber long before it was realized that the pods were edible and highly nutritious. Seeds may be sown outdoors when the danger of frost has passed but sowing in pots during spring provides a much larger plant more quickly. They may even be grown in pots or in hanging baskets where there is no room in the ground. Given adequate water they twine up canes or netting to form a dense screen of large, heart-shaped leaves with numerous spikes of scarlet, pink or white flowers. If the pods are picked regularly for the kitchen, the plants will flower over a long period.

PLUMBAGO capensis

Sadly, plumbago is hardy only in sub-tropical areas but it is easily grown in a greenhouse. Its gently rambling habit, soft green leaves and clusters of clear pale blue flowers are beautifully displayed in pots and window boxes but it can also be plunged in its pot or planted out into the garden during the summer to ramble through the flower border, looking wonderful with grey foliage and pink, white or pale yellow flowers.

RHODOCHITON volubile

Easily grown as a half-hardy annual, this fascinating plant produces dark green, heart-shaped leaves that twine their petioles around supports to grow rapidly upwards. It produces inflated buds of purple-maroon that open to reveal long deep maroon tubular flowers in every leaf axil. The colourful calyx remains after flowering, festooning the plant with deep purple bells.

Rhodochiton can be grown through the darker fuchsias to create a subtle blend of deep purples and reds. Its dusky flowers make a lovely contrast to the white daisies and silver grey leaves of *Argyranthemum frutescens foeniculaceum* or will brighten *Grevillea robusta*, jacaranda and other plants grown mainly for their foliage.

TROPAEOLUM peregrinum

Canary creeper
Closely related to climbing nasturtiums (*T. majus*), the canary creeper is more refined, with leaves that are grey-green, small and attractively lobed. They twine their petioles to scramble through netting or twiggy shrubs and, from late summer, produce cascades of bright yellow fringed flowers. It requires protection from blackfly and caterpillars.

Phaseolus vulgaris

INDEX

Page numbers in *italics* refer to illustrations

ACKNOWLEDGMENTS

Author's Acknowledgments

I should like to thank Frances Lincoln for inviting me to write *The Flower Garden*, and her team of skilful editors and designers for their enthusiasm. Photographs throughout the book are by Marijke Heuff, who deserves loud praises for her artistry and technical ability in capturing so well the evanescent moods of the flower garden. Thanks to Anne Fraser and Louise Tucker for their assistance in selecting illustrations and integrating them into the text.

The ideas expressed in *The Flower Garden* are my own, but they have been shaped by visits to hundreds of gardens over more years than I care to recall so I must thank the great fraternity of gardeners for the inspiration they give so generously.

Lastly, my most profound thanks go to my wife who so patiently took on a double dose of parental duty, slaved to keep our garden in order and did her best to keep the rest of the world at bay while I struggled at the typewriter.

Photographer's Acknowledgments

I should like to thank all my dear 'garden' friends who have made this book possible, whose gardens are for me oases of beauty where I find inspiration and creative energy.

Four gardens that open to the public regularly in the summer months are the gardens of Ton ter Linden in Ruinen, of Mien Ruys in Dedemsvaart, the Priona-gardens, Schuinesloot and Paleis Het Loo, Apeldoorn. Information about other gardens in the Netherlands is available from De Nederlandse Tuinenstichting (Dutch Garden Society), at Prinsengracht 624–626, 1071 KT Amsterdam.

Information about gardens in Great Britain is available from the National Trust, 36 Queen Anne's Gate, London SW1H 9AS. Hestercombe, the Gertrude Jekyll garden in Somerset, can be visited by appointment. Other gardens in England and Wales are open through the National Gardens Scheme, 57 Lower Belgrave Street, London SW1W 0LR.

Publishers' Acknowledgments

The publishers would like to thank the following individuals for their help in producing this book: Jo Christian; Paul Meyer for his horticultural advice; Peter Moloney for the index; Tim Foster for initial design work; Yvonne Cummerson for design assistance; and Katy Foskew for her cheerfulness and clerical skill:

Editors   Susanne Haines, Barbara Vesey
Art Editor   Louise Tucker

Art Director   Caroline Hillier
Picture Editor   Anne Fraser

Illustrators
Garden plans by Jenny Abbott (Garden Studio)
Cover border by Michael Craig

Photographs
Marijke Heuff

Typesetting
Set in Bembo by Bookworm Typesetting, Manchester, England

Origination
Evergreen Colour Separation Co. Ltd, Hong Kong